SECRETS TO FREE ADVERTISING ON THE INTERNET

SECRETS TO FREE ADVERTISING ON THE INTERNET

A COMPLETE COMPREHENSIVE GUIDE FOR LARGE AND SMALL
BUSINESSES ON HOW TO TAKE ADVANTAGE OF ALL THE FREE
ADVERTISING MEDIA AVAILABLE ON THE INTERNET

ROBERT NOLL & ANNE BRASHIER

New York

Secrets to Free Advertising on the Internet

A complete comprehensive guide for large and small businesses on how to take advantage of all the free advertising media available on the Internet

ISBN 978-1-60037-705-1

Library of Congress Control Number: 2009935983

Robert Noll
8275 S. Eastern Ave. #200-204
Las Vegas, NV 89123
888. 262. 6655
Sales@MonsterPPC.info

MORGAN · JAMES
THE ENTREPRENEURIAL PUBLISHER

Morgan James Publishing, LLC
1225 Franklin Ave., STE 325
Garden City, NY 11530-1693
Toll Free 800-485-4943
www.MorganJamesPublishing.com

In an effort to support local communities, raise awareness and funds, Morgan James Publishing donates one percent of all book sales for the life of each book to Habitat for Humanity. Get involved today, visit **www.HelpHabitatForHumanity.org.**

Table of Contents

About the Author vii

Introduction ix

SECTION 1: ONLINE LISTINGS

Chapter 1: Classifieds 3
    Where to list your business and how to list it so customers can find you

Chapter 2: Local Searches 15
    How to get locally connected in your community, your region, and your market

Chapter 3: Search Engines and Optimization 29
    Optimize your searchability with a well-designed website

SECTION 2: ONLINE CUSTOMER CONNECTIONS

Chapter 4: E-mail Marketing. 41
    What email marketing can do for you, and how to do it easily for free

Chapter 5: Blogging Basics 51
    An online business journal can be far more than just a little diary

Chapter 6: Feeds 65
    Extra, Extra! Let your customers read the latest about your company!

SECTION 3: SOCIAL MEDIA

Chapter 7: Business-to-Business Networking. 75
    Don't be a wallflower! Network online for free

Chapter 8: MySpace 85
    Getting socially connected on the Internet to expand your potential market

Chapter 9: Facebook 95
    Friendship online, and how it can help your company

SECTION 4: NEW MEDIA

Chapter 10: Mobile Marketing 109
Get your message directly into the hands of your customers

Chapter 11: Twitter. 117
An exciting new way to get your business buzzing!

Chapter 12: Videos 125
Lights, Camera, Your Free Online Ad!

SECTION 5: WHAT NEXT?

Chapter 13: Pay Per Click 139
Launch your business to the next level with targeted online ads

Chapter 14: What Next? 145
Technology keeps evolving, but we'll help you keep up!

Glossary 147

References 151

BONUS 153

About the Author

ROBERT NOLL IS AN EXPERIENCED and successful Internet entrepreneur, and a veteran in the Internet advertising field. Robert was born in Washington D.C., and raised in Allentown, PA. He has owned and operated a wide range of businesses and is now President and owner of Monster PPC in Los Angeles, CA.

A self-taught businessman, Noll has learned from experience how to grow a business and how to generate a profit. Choosing life experience over textbook knowledge, Noll has had great success as an independent entrepreneur in many fields.

Noll wanted to share his online marketing experience and expertise with business owners who might not be taking advantage of the power of the Internet. He noticed a void in the materials for average business owner about the wide range of marketing possibilities on the World Wide Web. This book is for business owners looking to expand their own marketing efforts. Not a highly technical manual, this book is accessible to the budding company or individual who wants to begin their media campaign on the Internet with little knowledge of computer programming.

Introduction

WHEN I FINISHED THE FIRST draft of this book, I emailed a copy to my youngest brother and asked for an honest read and review. A week later, I received a phone call from him while he was visiting New York City on a business trip. Without any hesitation at all he blurted out "It reads like a Hewlett Packard manual!" So I went back to the drawing board to try and insure that I accomplished two things: an interesting read and a learning experience. Hopefully with the assistance of a co-author and very capable editor I will achieve both of these goals. Quite frankly, it is a much more difficult task than I ever thought, but I will certainly give it my best shot.

Perhaps I should start by letting you know that although it would be best to read this book from start to finish, it is not necessary. You can just go to the chapter that you would like to utilize for your advertising campaign. Another of my brothers always says "life is about choices; the choices we make today affect what we become tomorrow." His logic certainly applies to advertising and marketing. So, I will suggest that you choose three or four of the title chapters and master them. You can't and shouldn't try to put all the strategies outlined in this book into practice at once. There are just too many avenues out there for you to follow, and the amount of information available to business owners can be overwhelming. If you attempt to follow them all, you will end up back where you started: nowhere.

Let's assume that you open a florist shop. Spending thousands of dollars advertising in the papers, in the phone book, on billboards, on radio, on television, and with fliers, you realize it's a necessity to advertise on the Internet as well. When people search online for flowers, you want your store's name to instantly appear in front of them. You want them to know exactly where you are and to get directions, to know your hours of operation, to understand your specialties, to see your prices, and even to be directed your website to make an order, or to set up an appointment. Now imagine you could do this all for free! Start by choosing three chapters from this book, for example, email marketing, classifieds, and blogs.

Using simple, step-by-step directions, <u>Secrets of Free Advertising on the Internet</u>, and its companion website <u>www.RobertNoll.com</u>, will show your new florist shop how to quickly advertise online for free. Even if you are not computer savvy, or you don't understand the complexities of Internet advertising, we explain everything from the Pay-Per-Click ins-and-outs, to how to set up classified ads, and how to get optimized for a local search.

Whether you own a florist shop, dentist office, law firm, etc., online advertising is a must if you want to grow and prosper. This book, <u>Secrets to Free Advertising on the Internet</u>, was written with an understanding of how fluid the Internet is, and how quickly it changes. When I started writing this book, there was no BING.com or GoogleWave, the two newest Internet players to know. With this constant evolution in mind, I have developed <u>www.RobertNoll.com</u> as your best resource to stay ahead of each next new online marketing trend. The website will help you organize and execute your advertising goals without having to spend hundreds of hours researching the latest online technology.

Searching Amazon Books for "Internet Advertising" reveals nearly 6,000 books. However, there are no books that explain how to begin an entirely free Internet advertising campaign. This is surprising, since according to PlunkettResearch.com there are 1.3 billion people using the Internet, and companies in the U. S. alone spend nearly 30 billion dollars on advertising.

With the ever-evolving Internet structure, this plethora of free advertising may not be around for long. Businessstrata.com reported that Market intelligence provider IDC research predicts total online marketing spending is set to reach $65.2 billion this year, and in three years is expected to reach $106.6 billion. People are paying to advertise, but That's not where most companies should start! This is the time to capitalize on what still remains to be free. <u>Secrets to Free Advertising on the Internet</u> will show you how!

This book is not to be confused with Guerrilla Marketing, which is "an unconventional system of promotions on a very low budget, relying on time, energy and imagination instead of big marketing budgets." <u>Secrets to Free Advertising on the Internet</u> will discuss free advertising that is offered primarily through blogs, classifieds, social networks, traffic exchange programs, and video advertising. There are books devoted entirely to Blogging, Social Networks, and Video Advertising, but nothing compiled into one guide. This book will show you, step by step, in easy to understand terminology, how to advertise for free, from opening a free account, to tracking your website's traffic. Instead of having to buy ten books on ten separate subjects and sifting through pages of unnecessary reading to get at what you're looking for, you will learn what you need to know in this in one publication.

Certainly, I wrote this book to help you and your company save money on advertising. But I do want to let you know that my specialty is Pay-Per-Click advertising, with my company goal being "the optimum number of qualified leads for the least amount of dollars spent." And I think some smaller companies should consider at least a limited budget for Pay-Per-Click advertising because of its Return on Investment and cost effectiveness.

I had often wondered why I liked Pay-Per-Click so much and why I excelled at it. It was my third brother who reminded me "It's because you grew up reading a racing form, where it's all about getting your horse to number one." Google AdWords is basically the same, and he's right; I always loved analytics, statistics, and winning!

So, whether you are a successful business owner, or someone who just started their first website, this book can save you thousands of dollars on advertising and give you a much needed head start in this extremely competitive virtual world. Now, let's roll!

SECTION 1:

ONLINE LISTINGS

THE NIELSON PARTNER WEBVISIBLE CONDUCTED an in-depth study on how small businesses fall into an odd trap online: they seek information on the Internet, but they fail to keep a strong online presence for themselves. Though 63% of consumers and small business owners turn to the Internet first for information about local companies and 82% use search engines to do so, only 44% of small businesses have a website[1]. So, the first step to getting your business to pop up in the top 10 search terms for any relevant keyword for your company is to have a good website! This should be a no-brainer by now; every company should have a website, from car repair shops to bakeries to financial consulting firms.

Once you start thinking of the Internet as one huge low-cost marketing tool to get buyers into your virtual "store," you'll find that you have thousands of ways to reach thousands of new customers, most of whom are interested in you and have already sought you out! In addition to a well-designed website, social networks, and pay-per-click banners, free online lists are a great way to stay in touch with clients. Not only that, if you don't take advantage of the millions of people who have Internet access, who check e-mails all day either on computers, mobile phones, or PDAs, you'll miss out on loads of business. So, let's get started!

Chapter 1:
Classifieds

I WAS A PAPERBOY, VERY briefly. Not a job I miss at all. But if I had to get up at 3am to load all the information now available online into my messenger bag, I would need a bigger bicycle! In fact, there is more information available to consumers online now than any newspaper could ever contain. Yet consumers still go to reliable sources on the web for practical information, like finding a landscaper or a plumber. That's why you have to get yourself listed in the most popular directories online.

It used to be that if you wanted to find a job or buy a car or hire a moving company, you checked the newspaper for classified ads. Now, you might still open the newspaper, but the odds are good that your potential customers do most of their searching online. Lucky for you there is a wide range of online classified sites that can offer listings for your company. There's a place for every type of service and product online, so no matter what your company has to offer, an online classified listing can work for you. Better yet, the majority of these sites are free!

Classifieds offer free listings for businesses and are one of the easiest ways to get leads matched perfectly to your demographic. We will show you how to list your company in online classifieds and discuss what to watch out for. We'll also discuss how this kind of advertising hits the biggest demographic range.

Almost all people using the Internet use this type of advertising. It is fast and effective, and leads the seeker to the exact product or service for which they are searching.

Just like the old-fashioned phone book or classifieds in the newspaper, online classifieds allow small companies to list their goods and services. Classifieds are great at targeting local and niche markets, putting your info right on the radar of consumers looking for your type of business. Since there is so much chatter on the Internet, this chapter will teach you how to get your ad noticed by the right people, and increase your return on investment.

WHERE TO LIST YOUR BUSINESS

The Internet is not an "if you build it, they will come" environment. Unless your ad is in the right location, no one will notice. So, here are a few tips for finding the best place for you to list your classified ad. You can also check out this book's up-to-date resource website, www.RobertNoll.com, for the latest classified site information.

A. Generic classified sites

An easy place to start getting your ad listed is to go to any of the wide range of general free classified sites on the web. YellowPages.com and WhitePages.com are two obvious classified listing choices, but there are many others. 411.com (the online equivalent of dialing 411 for Information) is another well-known directory you should join. Because these sites cover a very wide range of industries, and because they reach the largest demographic both geographically and individually, label your ad with as many specific keywords as possible. That way if you are a florist specializing in weddings, gifts, parties, deliveries, and roses, searches for all those words will bring up your company!

Some sites such as yellowpages.com offer you the chance to register with one company and get listed on numerous sites all owned or affiliated by the parent company. Superpages.com is a great place to start. On the Internet, your company's main objective should be to divide, multiply, and conquer!

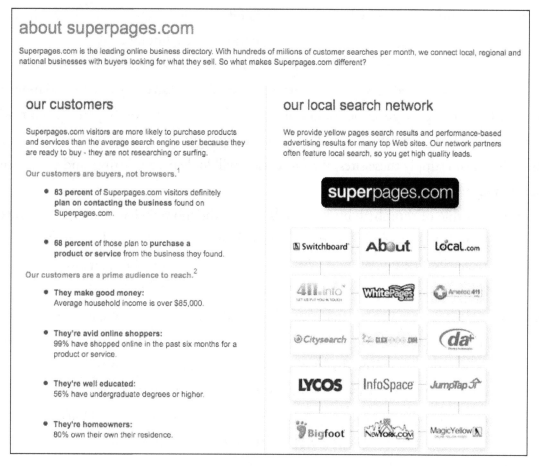

Figure 1.1: www.superpages.com

Here are the steps to signing up for Superpages.com. Most other large free classified websites have essentially the same company registration process.

1. Find out if your company already has a listing by entering your business phone number into the first field.

2. Add your business address and listing information, and your business category. If your business fits into more than one category, make sure you list them all.

3. Select the keywords that represent the specific brands, services, and products you offer.

4. List your hours of operation, your accepted methods of payment, and any relevant certifications, affiliations or company memberships.

5. Finally, list the area in which you want to offer service: are you a local store in a big city, or are you an online store offering nation-wide shipping?

Once you have signed up with your company e-mail, you can easily update and monitor your business listing. Registering for classified ads like the listings on Superpages.com will ensure that online shoppers can find your company right when they need it. The more information you supply these sites, the more users will look at your listing, and then spend their money with you!

A general rule of thumb about classifieds is this: the more review and verification the site requires to list your ad, the more professional and respected the ad site is. Most sites have strict rules about adult content (even increased fees) and for sites that violate security, FCC, and privacy codes. But let's assume that you've got a fully legit business, so now all you have to do is submit your ad and the link to your site, as well as company information, to the classified site and you are on your way. Once you have the ads up and running, you can easily track the click-throughs to your own homepage from each website with basic analytics on your own company website. You can also get a sense of the traffic a site gets by how quickly the listings change as you return to the site over a week. Don't be worried that your ad shifts position; that just means that you're on a highly trafficked site, which is always a good place to be!

B. Search engine classifieds

Over 75% of online searches use Search Engines, which means that when customers come looking for your business, this is a key place they start.[2] Yahoo, Google, and MSN all offer free classified ads and directories where you can list your business. Since these are three of the top Search Engines (see Chapter 2 for Search Engine info), they get millions of viewers a day, and some of those people are going to want and need what you have to offer. Different from getting your ad to pop up in the top 10 of a search (which we'll cover in Chapter 2), putting a sponsored ad on a major search engine will give you prime online real estate.

Google will list companies on classifieds both in alphabetical order and Page Rank order (the order that the search engine lists your site in a general search). The Google directory limits and enhances the general search capability of Google, and is based on the Netscape Open Directory Project (ODP). ODP volunteers sort through website submissions and select the most respected, legitimate, trustworthy websites to include in what is essentially an online reference library.

To get listed on Google's free classified directory, go to the Open Directory Project homepage, http://www.dmoz.org/add.html, and search to make sure that your website is not already listed. Then, once you verify that you fulfill all the other directory conditions (nothing illegal, no duplicate sites, no under-construction sites, etc.), pick the *single most relevant category* for your website. Finally, click "Submit URL" and wait for the editors to accept you.

The Open Directory Project's reference list is enormous, so a number of directory sites use it on their own search pages. This means that once you get on the ODP, you'll be automatically listed on the search lists for Google, Yahoo!, AOL, Netscape, and hundreds of others.

Yahoo! uses the ODP data for its classified lists, so you don't need to pay the hefty yearly fee to get listed on the Yahoo! directory. AOL lets you list for free, if you go to http://www.classifieds.aol.com/post/ and click on "Post a Free Ad!" Their list options are basic: 3 categories, your title and business description, your contact information, and your address. From there, they will email you a verification link for you to click through. It's fast, free, easy, and a great way to get your ad online.

MSN uses InetGiant.com to host its classifieds, so to get a listing on MSN and it's new search partner BING, go to http://www.inetgiant.com/PostNewAd.aspx. Select the "I am offering" button, and select your business category. The site will guide you through an easy process so you can narrow exactly how you are listed to the most accurate description. Then, add a description, title, 2 free photos, and all of your business information. The basic listing is free, though the website will push you to upgrade to more services at each step. Check each field carefully or you might be signing up for extra, unnecessary, and expensive services.

C. Craig's List

We've got to talk a bit about Craig's List, since it is the most multi-purpose international online classified site. Craig's List lets anyone list anything, from pets to pianos to plumbers. If you run a small local business this is a great place to get customers. Since Craig's List operates as more of a local site in thousands of cities and regions, small service providers such as nannies, plumbers, car repairmen, etc, can really focus local buyers on their service. Craigslist.org is not the best place to list your online clothing store, your electronic retail store, or your restaurant. But it can be a very useful place for small businesses to get attention from their local communities. Also, because the lists get updated so frequently, it's a great place for real estate agents to list properties: you can showcase individual homes, though there is a fee for real estate listings.

Because Craig's list is primarily moderated by the individuals or organizations posting ads, set yourself apart with your professionalism. A good example of a Craig's List posting is Figure 1.2, a makeup artist posting her services for hire. Her listing includes a link to her website, photo examples of her work, and a basic idea of what she has to offer.

Professional Makeup Artist (Travel to You!!)

please flag with care:
miscategorized
prohibited
spam/overpost
best of craigslist

Reply to: serv-rq3ew-1228173474@craigslist.org [Errors when replying to ads?]
Date: 2009-06-18, 12:45PM PDT

Professional makeup artist with over 5 years of experience. I have various celebrity and major international commercial clients, with current campaigns running in national media.

I also offer my services for weddings and other special events, like formals, anniversaries, etc. Available for private or group lessons & engagement photos. Airbrush, male grooming, tattoo cover, and other specialty services are also available! I offer both makeup and hair styling, will travel to your location!

See more work at www.allielapidus.com,. Please contact me at info@allielapidus.com for rates and availability!

Figure 1.2: www.craigslist.com makeup artist ad

Another great example of using Craig's List for your company is this ad for a muffler repair shop. The ad gives clear, detailed, concise information about what services they offer and how you can get in touch with them. They list their hours and staff, and overall they seem professional and helpful.

Figure 1.3: www.craigslist.com car repair shop ad

D. Industry-specific classifieds

The Internet is all about niche marketing, so the more specific you can be, the better. Find out which free classified sites are specific to your industry. Look at how quickly the top ads are changing on the site. And don't be afraid to check out the competition; a search of your competitors will reveal what other sites they use to list ads. Be sure to look at related industry sites and demographic specific sites. Do you offer furniture re-upholstering? Check out antique furniture classified sites. Running a small winery? There are endless food service, catering, and restaurant listings to get your ad on.

Often businesses that have mostly online services offer classified space on their websites; more on this in the affiliate deals section below.

The more a site relates to what you have to offer, the better click-through rate you will see when your ad is on that site!

FIRST IMPRESSIONS COUNT

The user has already expressed interest in what you have to offer. They have come to this ad list to find a travel agent or tire repair shop or veterinarian who is professional, cost-effective, and who fits their specific needs. Now you simply have to convince them that you are the perfect match!

Just like a first date with messy clothes, a poorly written classified ad can quickly put a stop to any future relationship. First impressions are critical in classified ads. You have only got a few words to entice the reader. It's critical that you spell everything correctly. Make sure you double or triple check your address, phone number, and website as they appear. Also, use plain English, and avoid Internet slang unless you feel it significantly adds to your company's brand.

Easy, right? Well, it takes a little effort, but once you have defined your company, once you have determined who would most benefit from your product or service, you can write up your ad and put it in the best places for prospective customers to find it. Now you need to think about whom you want to target and what specifically you want to promote in your classifieds. What sets your company apart from others like it? Remember, your ad will be in a long list of similar ads. Much like in creating e-mail subject lines, find what makes you stand out to grab the reader's attention!

Phrases that will help you stand out from the list are descriptions of your service: Speedy? Instant? Cheap? Luxury? Friendly? Expert? A little slogan like "Serving your community for 30 years" or "Service on time, every time" or "Service with a smile" placed right under your company name will let consumers know exactly what makes your company unique. Look at all the rest of your advertising and see what brings people back to your store. Are you conveniently located to a specific industry center? Do you offer a service that is trademarked and limited? Beyond your company name, a little tagline about the essence of your company can let consumers know a little more about what you have to offer them.

CHOOSING THE RIGHT WORDS

Classifieds are like e-mails, but even more succinct. Make sure your ad gets right to the point of what you want people to know about your company. Use keywords common to your industry so people can find you in a search. Also, use emotionally powerful words to get the reader excited. A little flattery goes a long way, so make the reader feel like she is being singled out for a limited VIP deal, or like he hunted down the perfect place to print business cards, buy plane tickets, etc. Again, these text-based ads are like e-mail subject lines, or, better yet, like pick-up lines on a first date.

Some classified sites charge by the line, but some charge by the word. If your classified service charges by the word, cut out any non-essential terms like "the," "an," or "thing." Be specific and focus on verbs, nouns, and adjectives to make an impact. The Google advertisers suggest including verbs in your ad so that readers are instantly encouraged to "buy" or "shop" or "eat" with you. Keep the tone pleasant and professional, and you'll be on your way to increased business in no time!

Be specific, concise, and, if you can, or if it's appropriate to your ad, be funny. But a word to the wise about humor: err on the side of caution. Never be off-color or vulgar, and resist the urge to be funny if it will make your business seem less professional. Consider what you want to emphasize about your company: Prompt Service? Experience? Low Cost? Friendly Customer Service? Any one of these can set you above the competition, so include these terms in your ad.

Some listing services allow you to include a logo or image, and these can certainly draw the eye. Often sites can give you a template to design your ad, list your ad, and give you tools to monitor the traffic to your site. But beware: these classified lists/ content service platforms frequently charge set-up fees for this additional feature, so be sure to go over their terms of service carefully. Most importantly, list your company name and contact info clearly and consider listing a phone number, physical address, e-mail address, and website. Make it easy for interested consumers to get in touch with you. Check out this book's companion website for some examples of effective classified listings.

WORKING WITH AFFILIATES

Online affiliate deals are even more effective than affiliate marketing in other media, because information is easily available to readers. When you get your ad on a larger marketing website, you get prime virtual real estate that can drastically increase your return on investment. Putting your name up on an affiliate site also lends authenticity to your company. The best sites to work with are service or product sites that reach the same demographic you want to capture. We'll go a bit more in depth in this when we discuss blogs, which offer free, but less guaranteed structured relationships. It's enough to say that affiliate marketing can create a solid online presence for your company.

The most commonly used form of affiliate compensation is Cost Per Sale, which allows both sides to share responsibility, risk, and loss. Cost per action/sale methods require that referred visitors do more than visit the advertiser's website before the affiliate receives commission. The advertiser must convert that visitor first. It is in the best interest for the affiliate to send the most closely targeted traffic as possible to the advertiser to increase the chance of a conversion. For more information on affiliate marketing, check out our companion website, www.robertnoll.com.

The best types of affiliations, therefore, are those that draw targeted customers to your site. Much in the same way that iTunes recommends songs you might like based on your music tastes, and Amazon recommends other purchases that people who like what you like buy, an affiliate should enhance what your brand is all about. Shopper comparison sites, budget finder sites, and coupon sites are great places to list yourself if deals and sales are a big selling point for your business. Customer loyalty sites and niche content sites are great if you have a luxury item or higher end service. Hit the right demographic and you'll be well on your way!

Once your company really expands its online presence, you might want to outsource your affiliate marketing to people who can keep up with what sites your ad should be on. Similar to traditional advertising agencies, these certified providers can help manage your online presence. Obviously this is a big next step, but it can help you join a large company affiliate with only those networks of the most benefit to you.

TIME SAVING LISTING TIPS

Here are a few business pointers to help you keep all your ads organized. Bookmark each page you put your ads on, or mark those sites as "favorites." Create several master templates for ads so that you can quickly put your ad up on a new site, or revise your ad to showcase new deals or specials. Even though this is all online, it's important to write down what ad you put on what site when.

Create urgency in your ads as well, and people will respond emotionally. When you limit the length of a sale or the number of items available at a reduced rate, you draw customers in. Classified ads are a great place to do this because you can easily update them, and people typically hunt on classifieds for convenience.

One of the reasons online classified ads are so effective is that it is easy to search them for a wide range of terms. Users can find you not just by your company name or your product type, but also by your phone number, address, specific promotion, catch phrase… anything they know about what you have to offer can lead them quickly to you. So, if you are looking for a catering service focused on weddings near the beach, online classifieds can lead you directly to the right company. Another plus of online classified ads is their longevity. As opposed to running a one-line periodical ad for one day, online sites typically offer rates per week, and allow much longer copy. Also, having your ad online allows you to modify it quickly and easily.

CLASSIFIED PITFALLS TO AVOID

If a site charges you a listing fee, maintenance fee, or set-up fee, stay away! These sites want your money upfront and cannot promise you returns. The exception is for real estate or job listings: many sites charge either a basic listing fee, or smaller sites charge for these ads because of the high turnover for both of those categories. Decide if this is right for you or not.

Make sure the site you put your ad on allows the browser to click through to your website (if your company does not have a website, get one now!). If the site does not allow this, don't even bother.

Some sites promise to put your ad on the top of their list every two hours, or promise a certain number of click-throughs per day. These sites are probably not viewed by many people, so don't waste your time. Get your ad out where people actually go to find it.

Beware of sites that promise exact returns! You want actual leads, and those leads come from putting your ad on highly trafficked sites. Again, find out how much traffic a site gets by checking the site several times to make sure a variety of ads pop up. Word of mouth can be a great way to find which sites to list on as well. Talk to others in your industry, or to affiliate partners to see which sites they go to!

Chapter 2:
Local Searches

REMEMBER THE DAYS WHEN YOU found out about a new business in your town by driving around and noticing the "Grand Opening" sign? The days of scanning the phone book and calling 411 are slipping away quickly. Now when I want to find a lawyer or doctor in my neighborhood, I search the Internet. And I'm not the only one!

Once you've got a company website, now is the time to put it where users can find it. Here is where a wide variety of free local search portals come in.

Maybe you have experienced the wonders of local search. Been waiting in line for coffee too long? Pull out your wireless PDA and search for another café in the vicinity. Sitting at home on a Saturday night? Order pizza and a video directly through the Web (and while you're there, become a fan of your local pizza joint on Facebook!). What's good for the searcher is even better for the search-savvy local business owner. Even if your organization doesn't have a brick-and-mortar component, you should have a website, and consumers in your area can't seek you out if you're not even on the radar!

Local search isn't just for people living in a certain region; it's also a huge aid to travelers. Say you have to travel to a new city, and you know you'll need a hotel, rental car, a nice restaurant, a cheap lunch place, a floral shop for a gift, and a watch repair store, since you didn't have time to get that nice watch fixed before rushing out the door and onto the plane. You could get a long list from the hotel concierge when you get in from your flight, exhausted. Of course, that's after you found a hotel at the airport, pressured for time. A simple search online can allow you to quickly find the best vendors for all your needs.

In this chapter we'll go over the basics of how to market your business through local searches. There are a number of different sites where people can search for businesses they need. This is great because right from the start, the consumer sought you out!!! So, if you're easy to find, local searches can reap enormous returns.

Worried that your business won't have the online national recognition of a larger brand? Well, local search is where the internet is your friend: being a small business is a huge asset in local searches, especially if you are in a boutique industry. Frequently, if people are traveling to a new place, they'll search online for the spots that their destination has to offer. So set yourself apart from national chains with reviews and recommendations from other local sites and start a local network!

The major search engines offer local searches by map-specific sites and within standard listings for certain searches. For example, type Boston bakery into Yahoo!, and at the top of the screen, you'll see prominently featured local results. Wouldn't it be nice to be listed there, maybe even with some sizzling five-star reviews next to your company name? Here's how to start.

HOW TO GET LOCAL

1. Make your website stand out

Put your physical address and contact info (phone number, hours of operation) on every page of your website. Again, make yourself easy to find: the web allows users to filter through a large amount of data at lightening speed, so you had better stand out and make yourself very accessible once people find you. If your website's main job is to drive walk-in traffic, be sure to include your business address and phone number on all pages of the site. This is easy to accomplish using a footer or template, and sends the search engines a strong message about your location. Include variations of your locality keywords (such as "WA" and "Washington"), and don't forget the importance of neighborhood names. If your business operates out of several locations, create a separate landing page for each spot.

Even if your company has a mainly online or virtual business, you can't be included in a local search unless you list a clear address. The search engine crawlers will pick up your tags. You can also include a map widget on your website (Mapquest, Yahoo! and Google all offer this API), which increases your rank in the search engines and gives your site and your business more legitimacy.

2. Register your site locally

According to an SBI+M article, 54 percent of Americans have substituted the Internet and local search for phone books[3]. Ninety percent of online commercial searches result in a local offline purchase and 61 percent of all local searches results in a transaction. According to an industry press release, online yellow pages usage is growing with each year. Better yet, the majority of yellow pages searchers are reported to actually follow through with an in-store visit!

To register your site on local search sites, go to such a site as www.citysearch.com or www.local.com. Go to the "advertise with us" or "Own your own business" section on these sites.

Then, go to the "find your business" section, and enter in your address, or your company name, or phone number. If you are already listed, great! Just fill in the rest of your information. If you're not on any of the search sites, enter in as many fields as you can:

Company name

Business address

Phone number and fax number

Email address

Company website URL

Business description

Products, services and brands you offer

Hours of operation

Accepted payment methods

Languages spoken

Number of locations

Number of employees

Discounts offered (AAA, military, student, senior, etc.)

Remember that any specialty you have, anything that can set you above the competition, needs to be on your listing. Maybe you are a female-owned business in a male-dominated industry, or you offer same-day service, or you have easy parking, or a play area for kids while customers wait. Whatever your little extra service is, make sure people know about it.

Most online yellow pages sites have some form of free business listing available. So, submit to all the free directories, which are more permanent than classifieds. Local.com, yellowpages, localeze, and infoUSA are all great, highly used sites on which you should get listed right away.

But beware: these websites all offer pricier, more featured listings, and frequently it's easy to click through a page and find yourself signed up for months of paying for your ad. Read all the fine print carefully when you register your site.

FIND YOUR NICHE IN YOUR COMMUNITY

Online marketing is all about personalizing the user experience so the consumer feels in control of the interaction. Think about all the types of people that might use your product or want your service; the fact is, there is a local or small search site for all of them. Consumers will be specific about what they are seeking (Brooklyn day spa offering aromatherapy, rare bookstore in Chicago), so make your tags specific on your site. Also, seek out what sites your consumers might visit to get information, and make sure your company is listed, in detail, on those sites.

Get linked up locally with your better business bureau, chamber of commerce, union and guild sites, and any other network of businesses you can find relevant to your area. Make sure locals and town newcomers can find you. Remember, people who are in your area may be looking for your service for the first time, but tourists and newcomers might also want to know the fastest dry cleaning place or where to get a fake tan. Listings on local hotel websites and "things to do in your city" websites can really boost your business.

Listing your company on an industry-specific search engines is also useful. Local sites not only offer a map-based aggregate of businesses under a certain search heading, but they also offer basic reviews of the companies. Particularly if you offer a service and people might want to know where the best doctor in 5 miles of them is, they might go to Angie'sList.com or a health insurance website. If you're a restaurant, check out if you are on Chowhound. com, Yelp.com, and other search sites for local listings. Create a listing for yourself if you're not already on these editorial search sites. If you are listed, see what people are saying about you, fill in any info gaps, add pictures, and make your listing stand out. When you are on a local search site, people will be able to find you and make an informed decision about your company based on the reviews you are encouraging your customers to make about you!

GET NOTICED ON THE BIGGIES

First, find out if you're already listed, and see what info is out there on your company already. Surf the major search engines' local sites Yahoo! Local, Google Maps, and MSN Live Local to see if your business already has a listing. If no listing exists, or if yours needs an update, it's free for you to make the listing yourself.

On the major search engines you will need to get an account for your business to be listed in the local listings. Use your company's e-mail account (you have one, right?) for each site: you'll need a Google, Yahoo!, and MSN mailing address, all of which you'll want to check regularly for updates.

A. Google

At the moment, Google rules the search engine world. A survey of 1,000 Internet users in the United States by S.G. Cowen & Co. found that the longer people have been using the Internet, the more likely it is that Google will be their search engine of choice[4]. These frequent Google users are more likely than people who use competing search engines to have household incomes above $60,000.[5] Google is also the most popular search engine: 52 percent of respondents chose it as their primary site for general Web searches[6]. Google targets the high-earning, high-tech movers and shakers. If you've got a new gadget or a high-end service, Google's search engine is vital real estate. Here is what you need to know about how Google ranks sites, and how to get your company website on the right lists.

To get your business listed on Google, first log into the Google local listing homepage with your Gmail account. If you don't have a Gmail account, go to gmail.com and create an email account for your company, preferably yourcompanyname@gmail.com. The webpage for Google local listings is http://tinyurl.com/3a8sh4, which you can also link to from www.RobertNoll.com.

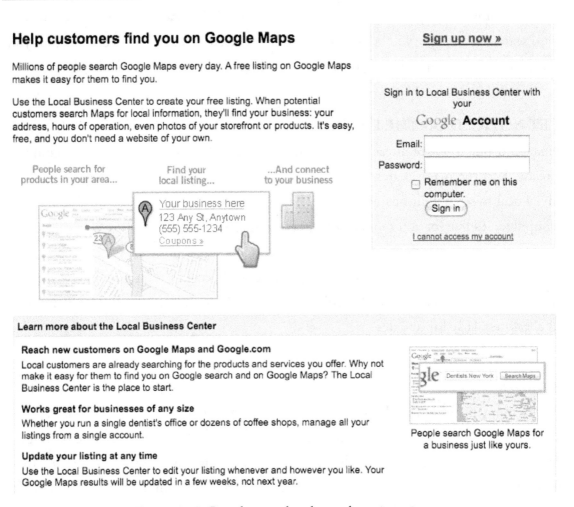

Figure 2.1: Google.com local search registration

From here, fill in all the Local Listing Sign Up fields, both the required and optional fields. The more information you fill out, the more your listing will stand out from other similar companies.

Required Fields:

Personal Information:

First/ Last Name

Phone Number

E-mail

Business Information:

Business Name

Business Address

Business Phone

Optional Fields:

Toll Free Phone Number

Fax Number

Web Address and Description

Business E-mail Address

Supplemental Phone Numbers

Hours of Operation

Payment Methods Accepted

Photographs- these are a great addition!

Year the Company was established

Company Tagline

Business Description

Brands and Products carried

Specialties

Professional Affiliations and Certifications

Languages Spoken

Parking Options

Professional Contacts

3. Add up to 6 categories that describe your business
4. Review Ad to ensure that all the information is correct and that the map shows your correct location
5. Complete the Service Agreement between yourself and the search engine
6. Verify your listing with the e-mailed confirmation code that they will send to you. After they have verified your business, your listing will start appearing on any one of these major search engines within 24 hours! And remember, you can modify your listing at any time.

Google has a wide range of functions, which means that your business can pop up all over the site if you tag your website well. Do not underestimate the power of Google video and image search. Make your site multi-media and people will be able to find you in a wide range of different places. For instance, if your site has a catchy video that gets passed around via word of mouth, people might search for the description of the video even if they can't remember your company name. But they'll end up being directed to your site just the same if you add your website URL to the video.

Blogger, Friendster, Picassa, YouTube, Google Maps are all part of the Google family, as are targeted searches for shopping, scholarly articles, and groups. Their Local Business Center allows you to put your company address, phone number, hours, website, and other details on Google Maps for free! You can even offer coupons for your services that people can print out and bring in. On your map listing, you can post photos and videos as well as reviews about your business. This is invaluable. And, any time you increase your web presence, you get a better search engine rank. Win win!

B. Yahoo!

Yahoo! started as "Jerry and David's guide to the World Wide Web!" and has become one of the leading global Internet communications companies. Yahoo! Search began as a directory of other websites, but that became limiting. By 2003 Yahoo! became its own scrolling search engine with the same ability as Google to hunt down information on the World Wide Web. Yahoo also focuses searches on images, video, shopping, news, and local results. It's definitely the number 2 player, but they are really putting effort into their development, and they are not going away yet!

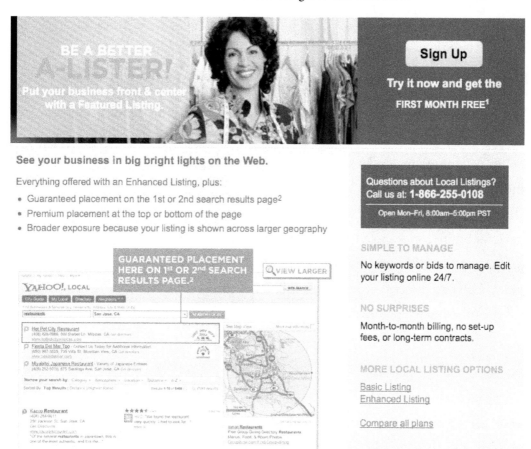

Figure 2.2: Yahoo.com local search directory

The Yahoo! Directory is a great resource for companies, so go to the Yahoo! homepage and search all the services they offer to businesses. From banners to pay-per-click ads, sponsored searches and ad design, Yahoo! has a variety of ways to help your business get online attention. To Join the Yahoo! local listing:

1. Go to http://listings.local.yahoo.com/basic.php, and click the "Sign Up" button for the Basic (free) listing

2. Log into your Yahoo! account with your email and password

3. Enter all the relevant information about your business (remember, the more detail you provide, the more customers you will attract)

      Your name

      You company name

Company address, phone number, email address, website

Hours of operation

Languages spoken, years of service, brand names carried, etc.

4. Fill out which master category and sub-category describes your business

You can have several different secondary categories to cover all of your service offerings. If you list your company under several category headings, you give customers more chances to find you.

Then, preview your listing with the map and all the attached information. Ask clients for reviews online, so you can start adding stars next to your listing. A good review on an online list can make an enormous difference when consumers are selecting a service provider. Also remember that you can update and edit your listing at anytime on Yahoo! or any of the other search engine sites.

MSN/ BING

Microsoft's Network is used by business professionals all over the world, and its industry standard carries credibility. Since MSN's homepage is a huge portal of information, people come to the site several times a day for news updates, e-mails, weather, and business news. When you register your website with MSN, you get access to Webmaster Tools. This helps you to design your site for optimum searchability, to check out what indices you are on, and to view statistics about your website's traffic.

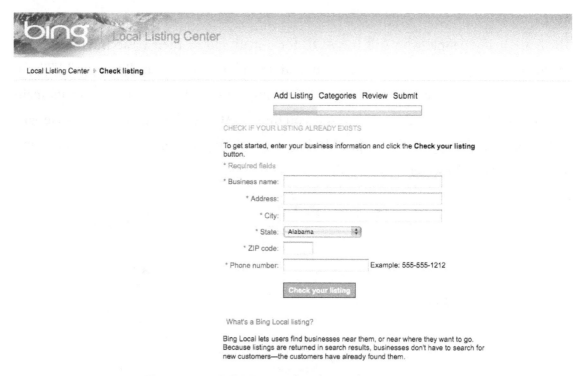

Figure 2.3: BING.com local search registration

Recently, Microsoft made a huge move forward into the search engine field with the development and release of BING. With a whole different approach to listing layout and advertising space, Microsoft is really trying to put itself above Google as the leading search engine. However, MSN's got an uphill battle, since people are already joking that BING stands for "But It's Not Google." Still, even if they only pick up a few points of the search engine market, it is worth your time and effort to have a presence here.

For MSN: https://ssl.search.live.com/listings/BusinessSearch.aspx Unlike its two counterparts, MSN uses a 3rd party — Verizon's Superpages.com — to provide paid advertising listings. Those listings then appear on MSN searches as well as BING searches. So, register on one site, get listed on several sites, all for free!

AOL

There are many people who still use AOL for e-mail and as their basic Internet service provider. As of September 2008, AOL still had 48 million users according to Bill Wilson, the AOL executive vice president for programming. But AOL has turned over its main search capabilities to Google, so the results you find on AOL will be the same as on Google. AOL does use their own crawling, indexing, and ranking systems for video, news, and shopping listings, however.

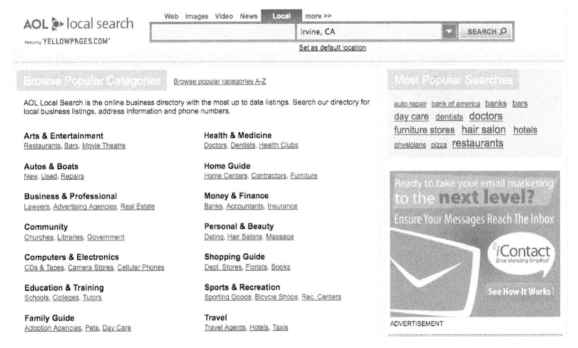

Figure 2.4: AOL.com local search listings

AOL is also linked with Mapquest, Moviefone, and Yellow Pages, so if you are on all these sites you will be easy to find. Most importantly, since AOL uses Google's search engine, as long as you are in Google's index, you'll also show up on AOL.

From the website access you get with this book, you can go to www.RobertNoll.com and find direct links to these pages. Check www.yourseoplan.com for other submittal URLs. The website for our book is a great resource for you as you expand your online marketing platform. As Search Engines and Classifieds evolve, you can continuously refer back to our website for the latest news about Internet advertising.

MAKE YOUR LISTING WORK FOR YOU

Be sure to get the most bang for your buck, so to speak, on these free local search listings. Fill in all the extra information you can: hours of operation, languages spoken, your website, multiple locations, and all fax and phone numbers. When all this info is in one place, people feel like they are in good hands, and they'll be more likely to go to your site, and then to your store.

Beautify your listing. Your listing needs some bling! It's easy to upload photos on Google, Yahoo!, or MSN, so why not give your local search surfers one more reason to visit your business? Photos of menu items or products, a downloadable brochure, or video testimonials can all be part of your local listing.

Last but not least, several of the major search engines offer you the ability to add a coupon to your listing, so when people scroll over your entry on a map, they not only see your info, they see that if they mention this ad, they get a deal! This is a great way to stand out from the 20 other t-shirt shops in your neighborhood.

Once you've done all this, remind one of your adoring customers how much you'd love a review. These reviews are priceless. Some companies can even offer discounts to repeat customers if they leave a positive review on a search engine. Since anyone can comment on you, regularly go back and do damage control in case something goes wrong. A little comment of apology after a bad review goes a long way toward showing you care- and it's a very public display of great customer service. A couple of stars behind your name and people feel they can trust your company a bit more. Since the odds are good that they are not able to check your place out in person or window shop, you have to make what you have to offer clear and appealing.

A final word about online marketing: if you cut down a virtual tree in the middle of the Internet woods, and no one hears about your amazing new axe, no one will buy one! Make yourself stand out by anticipating customer needs. With local searches, because people are already looking for someone just like you right in your neighborhood, a little effort to pop out makes a huge difference.

Chapter 3:
Search Engines and Optimization

I HAVE RUINED SEVERAL SATURDAYS trying to run errands before searching on the Internet became the most convenient way to find information. I would drive to a clothing store to find that they were out of my desired brand, then to a fax and copy shop only to find that I needed to go to a separate shop to print photos, and then having to find a photo printing shop, only to arrive at the hardware store an hour after they closed because I didn't know their weekend hours. Sure, good planning could have helped me, but my point is that the Internet can make planning much easier for consumers. So think about your business model from your consumer's point of view. Be easy to find, and they will more likely find you!

Search Engines have radically changed how consumers obtain and compare information. If I run an electronics repair store, I want my store's name to pop up everywhere on the Internet, every time a consumer in my area looks for repairs, electronics, electronic repairs, used electronics, radios, blenders, appliances, used appliances, and things to help them fix things. I also want them to find me if they search for a particular brand or style of any of the items I am able to fix. Bottom line, I don't want to play hide and seek with my potential customers.

The 11th edition of the Merriam Webster Collegiate Dictionary makes it official: Google is now a verb. Whereas most words take at least a decade to get in the dictionary, Google made the cut in only 5 years! There were almost 9 billion searches a month in the US done during 2008, with Google garnering about 70 % of these, or over 6 billion searches alone. Yahoo had 1.5 billion searches, MSN 850 million, and AOL 360 million[7]. This chapter shows you how to advertise for free on Google, Yahoo, MSN, and AOL, the four most important search engines on the Internet today. Millions of dollars of free advertising are available with these sites, yet so few people are taking advantage of this. Learning how search engines find websites can help you understand not only how important they are, but also how to use them to your company's advantage.

A search engine does two major tasks: it searches the Web for key words and combinations of key words, and it creates enormous indices of where those terms are found so it can easily relocate those pertinent sites. All search engines do this in some method, but then each search engine decides to list their findings in unique ways depending on the site's search algorithm. Today, a top search engine will index hundreds of millions of pages, and respond to tens of millions of queries per day. The more frequently a search engine gets used, the better it becomes at finding sites everyone else thinks are relevant to a query.

To find results, a search engine sends out virtual "spiders" into the World Wide Web. These "spiders" crawl through popular sites with heavily trafficked servers, indexing the search terms and any other frequently used, related words. Being the top name on a major search engine list is an elusive goal, because it is a huge attention-grabber. Frequently, people only look at the first page of a search if they find the right types of terms, even if there are thousands of matching results on other pages. You want to be at the top of the list, not somewhere lost in the middle.

I know what you're thinking: how can I get my company to come to the top of the list for several search keywords? Well, Search Engines use complicated rubrics to determine result listings, and they are pretty secretive about their exact formulas, since each site determines rankings differently. This is why your company can come up in different listing order on Yahoo, Google and MSN. The formulas all involve how many sites your site links to and how many link to it, how often people visit your site, and where else on the Web your name is mentioned.

The algorithm, or formula, for putting websites in order on the result list is a closely kept trade secret for search engines. Since top search listing is basically great free advertising, search engines want to maintain unbiased results. Google's PageRank™ system computes not just how many times a keyword appears on a page, but factors in over 200 signals about a site in a complex (and secretive!) algorithm to get the listing order. Some of those signals include:

o   Keywords and Tags

o   Links to and from your site

o   Traffic volume and frequency

o   Type of traffic

o   Website update frequency

All of these search engines, along with Ask.com, offer similar services for small businesses. They all host blogs about their constantly changing search systems, and make it easy to get in contact with tech departments. Though they won't tell you exactly how to get the number one spot on a search result list, they can help your site get the attention it deserves. However, you've got to do some of the work yourself when you get your website designed. In order to make your site stand out to these search engines, which are constantly crawling through millions of websites, you have to optimize your site.

Here's how.

OPTIMIZE YOUR SEARCHABILITY

Search Engine Optimization is what large companies do these days to get their names to pop to the top of search lists. You might hear the terms Black Hat, White Hat, Grey Hat Search Engine optimization (SEO) methods. White Hat methods are the legal ways to boost your list ranking, Black Hat ways are not legal, and Grey hats are somewhere in between. Here are some White Hat methods to make your company website easy to find.

1. Register your site on all major search engines.
    This is easy to do by going to any search engine homepage:
       For Google, go to http://www.google.com/addurl/
       For Yahoo!, go to www.siteexplorer.search.yahoo.com/submit
       For MSN, go to http://search.msn.com/docs/submit.aspx

From the website access you get with this book, you can go to www.RobertNoll.com and find direct links to these pages. Once you are here, the process for each search engine registration is similar to the process for local search registration. *Remember* that you are just registering your company on these websites, not buying pay-per-click or sponsored ads. Focus on free advertising first, to give your company a leg up on the competition.

Once you are at each company's search engine registration webpage, follow the same registration steps as for local search, and keep in mind that the more information you give, including reviews, coupons, photos, parking info, the more your listing stands out above the competition.

Trustworthiness is critical online. Attaching your company to a respected company can make you stand out in the immense amount of information available online. Since so much happens online without tangible feedback, and you can't ever really know where information comes from, the more you connect your company with reputable websites, the more potential customers will trust your company. Like good word of mouth, or a solid endorsement, getting your site officially registered with the major search engines adds credibility to your business.

2. Make keywords KEY.

A search scans the Internet for sites containing matching keywords, so your website had better be full of all relevant possible keywords someone could use to find your business. If you run a podiatry office, make sure you use the word "podiatry" several times on your webpages, as well as "foot doctor", "foot care", "healthy feet", etc. If you only use your trademark name, people might not remember to search for that exact thing. So even if you sell the Chopmaster200, the terms "blender" and "food processor" better be on your site.

For a good example of a small company maximizing searchability, LA foot and Wellness Doctor, a small practice with offices in Glendale, West LA, and Fairfax, consistently gets to the top of the list for several search terms, including LA foot Doctor, Glendale Foot Doctor, and Foot Wellness LA.

A warning on this: make the terms relevant to your site, and cohesive within the text. Spam sites and virus sites frequently consist of just lists of popular search terms, and search engines know to avoid listing these sites in results. Don't be one of these sites! So, fill your page judiciously, but avoid over-tagging and stuffing the page with key words.

Another use of keywords is in the tags on your website: these are the work of the programmer/ coder/ developer of your site. Whether you do this personally, or you hire someone to design your site for you, be clear that the HTML code reflects what you want your site to emphasize.

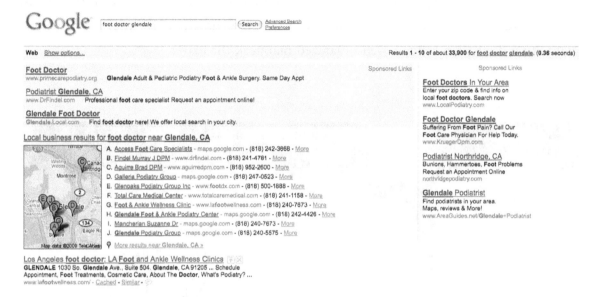

Figure 3.1: Google.com search results for LA Foot Wellness Clinic

3. Make your site easy to find.

Don't forget the importance to site design in relation to key words. Search engines don't just check for keywords; they also look for where the words are placed and how they are used. They pay more attention to keywords within the format of the page using important words in headings and titles. The best searches either rank for the correlation between content and title, or by including all the terms on the page to ensure cohesiveness within the site.

Include live links to maps and details of all your locations. Have searchable media, like images and videos, on your site. That way, the search engines have many ways of finding you. Google, for instance, has separate searches for images, video, and shopping. For a good example of a website with a wide range of features to increase searchability, see www.lafootwellness.com.

One fun tip for increased searchability is to make sure to include all the staff names and your bigger clients, so that when web users search for their former coworkers or follow influential trendsetters, they'll stumble upon your blog. Did you just do the landscaping for a public library or the house of a prominent business owner? Tag it! Do you have a staff with widely diverse backgrounds and interests (a designer, a secret musician, a former track star?) Tag it! You can never tell what will lead people to your site, so the more information you put up there (in a concise, well-organized manner), the better.

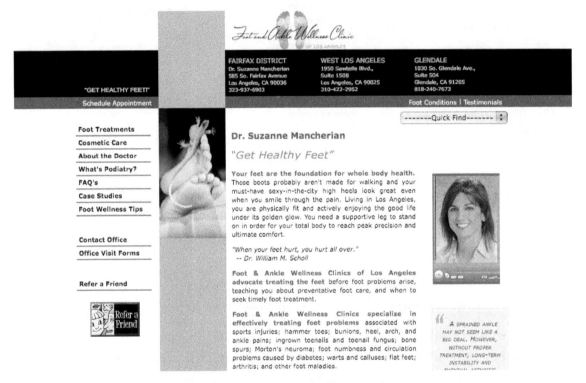

Figure 3.2: LA Foot Wellness website

4. Link up with others.

Search engines assign a higher rank to sites that are mentioned in other sites. So, if your site is mentioned on a very heavily trafficked site, such as a popular restaurant review site or health journal, and your website's URL is on their page, your rank will increase. Search engines also give higher ranking to pages that link to several other sites, though this is not quite as big a factor. The logic for this is that any site can link to a wide range of sites (sites that do this are actually called "link farms"), but if lots of websites link to you, they all recognize your importance. A good way to get specific links to your site is to award other websites that take actions toward causes your company supports. For instance, if you are a running apparel store, awarding "inspiring runner of the month" to relevant blogs can build your community. Or, if you are a theatre where tourists go, link to local restaurants to suggest dining options.

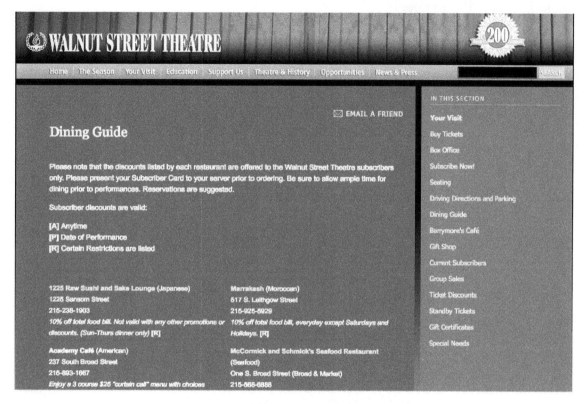

Figure 3.3: Walnut Street Theatre website

Get yourself some good virtual karma by building relationships like these informal affiliations. Generally, if you link to that person's website on your site, and feature them, they will likely link to you as well.

5. Know when you're in the press.

Online press releases from multiple sources increase your status on search engines, so if you have the chance to be seen in another media outlet, with a radio interview or article about your company on another website or print publication, seize it! The more coverage your company gets from other sources, even blogs and reviews, the higher your search engine ranking will be. Even if you are busy, take a few hours each week to search for your own company name or names of the brands, products you sell, or search your community or your industry. If there's anything out there relevant to your company, post a comment about it, link to it, promote it!

Figure 3.4: Top to Top running store website

6. Keep your site current.

It can be easy, once you set up your company website, to let it sit there, especially if you don't do a lot of online business (say you're a car mechanic shop, or a childcare center). But the search engines send out their "spiders" to crawl the Internet all the time! They are always out there, seeking changing and new information. So, if you update your site on a regular basis, by having a blog, or chat room, or calendar, or photo booth, whatever, your site will attract more attention.

HOW TO TRACK YOUR PROGRESS

Once you register your site, either as a sponsored or non-sponsored site, all of the major search engines have tools to show you who visits your site, where they come from, and what they do when they get there. Google's built in analytics track how often people come to your site, and if they come there via e-mails, links to other sites, searches, or on their own. Yahoo! Web Analytics is still being developed, but it can offer real time feedback about what people do on your site: which pages get the most traffic, what products people buy, and how they found your site. Web Analytics is a newly developing field, but one that will be increasingly useful to online businesses and advertisers. Google and Yahoo! offer these tracking services for free to sites registered with them. It's an easy way to get instant feedback about the online portion of your business. That way, you can make changes and see what happens, maximizing your web traffic.

SPONSORED SEARCHES

Google, Yahoo, MSN, AOL, and all the other search engines out there offer sponsored searches for your company. You can submit your info much like you would to a directory or classified site, but this pulls up your company info on the search term page. However, all these major sites separate regular search results from sponsored search ones. This can be great because if someone looks online for any info about, say, baby food allergies, and you have paid for a sponsored listing of your baby-clothing store, your company name will pop up in a special highlighted section!

The drawback here is that a regular search attempts to list results in an unbiased way. Basically, large search engines operate like the best word of mouth community: if a lot of Internet users think your company is the best match for what you're looking for (say, "downtown Los Angeles dress boutique"), they go to your site the most, so your site pops up on the top page of the search list. But sponsored searches are clearly advertising, and Internet users can be anti-advertising! Also, sponsored searches charge you by click-through. If you want to get ranked high for free, make good use of the Search Engine Optimization strategies listed above, as well as those found at our reference website, www.RobertNoll.com!

Think of your site a bit like a flower in a meadow. If your site is in a part of the meadow with lots of bees, and near other tasty flowers, and it looks and smells delicious, lots of insects will go to it. Similarly, if your site is easy to find, has reputable connections to other sites, and is an active part of your business, the search engine "spiders" will attract customers to you. Searches can offer the largest payoff with the least amount of work!

SECTION 2:

ONLINE CUSTOMER CONNECTIONS

CONNECTING WITH CUSTOMERS ONLINE CAN take many forms. The online listing options described above allow consumers to find you. But you might want to get pro-active and seek out or make contact with consumers via the World Wide Web. Emails and blogs are two wonderful ways to do this for free!

These days, everyone has email, and few people could go a day without checking their electronic in-boxes. And blogs (a web log, or online journal) are not just for over-emotional teenage diaries. Several multi-national companies host blogs, and some CEO's and leading political and financial figures write very popular blogs. Get up to date or be left in the dust!

Emailing and blogging about your company can give consumers more personal connection to your brand. Just like mailing out your company news letter or sending personalized holiday cards, keeping in touch with your clients builds their loyalty. The Internet makes it easier than ever before to stay connected to a wide market!

Chapter 4:
E-mail Marketing

TODAY I FOUND OUT THAT I qualified for a PhD, won the Nigerian Lottery, and was pre-approved for an instant $7,500 Platinum card. I also learned that I could have the secrets to the Oprah Diet. I'm really not sure I want that! Ah, the love/hate relationship we have with e-mails and e-mail campaigns. Even though we loathe spam, try turning your e-mail account off for a week, or even a day. How long do you think you would last?

Virtually every business, from accounting firms to zoos, should collect e-mails for further customer development. Let's take an example: you call your favorite local Italian restaurant to make a reservation. Here, the thoughtful hostess says, "Mr. Noll, may I have your e-mail address to confirm your reservation?" Sure, without hesitation, even though I know I will receive an e-mail from them for every holiday feast, menu change, or new vodka they discover. But do I mind? No. I actually look forward to these e-mails, and they remind me about a business I enjoy patronizing.

First, we'll take an in-depth look at what e-mail marketing can do for your company. Then, we'll outline several different ways to implement an e-mail marketing campaign. Finally, we'll help you figure out what to do once you've pressed send.

WHAT E-MAIL MARKETING CAN DO FOR YOU

If you're still not convinced that you should start e-mail marketing, you should know that 60 % of consumers make purchases based on e-mail marketing, and that for every $1 spent on e-mail marketing, a company gains $48 in revenue[1]. But before you start e-mailing, make sure you know why, what you want to get from your readers, and how you want them to make contact with you and your company. E-mail campaigns are useful for a variety of different businesses. Whether you want to sell products online, keep patrons updated on your services, or invite customers to in-store promotions, e-mail marketing can work for you.

Like any other marketing tactic, e-mail marketing has its pros and cons. But I'm confident you'll find that the challenges posed by embracing new technology far outweigh the cost you face if you don't jump on the e-mail superhighway, and soon.

E-mail Pros:
1. Adds value to your company by increasing client contact.
2. Encourages more frequent repeat business by keeping your brand in the minds of consumers.
3. Opens a dialogue with your customers so they can interact with you as much or as little as they want about services tailored to their needs.
4. Reduces operating costs by:
   allowing customers with service questions to seek information themselves, then to e-mail service centers, reducing pressure on call centers;
   reducing paper, printing, and mailing costs;
   reducing the need for storage space if products are available online.

E-mail Cons:
1. E-mailing customers takes time and discipline. Knowing how often to contact clients and what to include in e-mails are key to keeping customer loyalty.
2. Increased e-mail usage and the concurrent increase in spam can make it difficult to get e-mails through. (We'll show you ways to avoid spam blockers on page 48).
3. You must adapt to e-mails as an integrated marketing strategy not only consistent in your online presence (e-mails, website, banner ads, social marketing, etc.) but also from one media to the next (print, in-store, broadcast).

The bottom line is that e-mail allows you to make customer service more personal; *take advantage of this*! When you build a relationship with customers or potential customers by showing them products that match their interests, notifying them of deals that are right for them, or providing them with information particular to products they have already purchased, you build customer loyalty on a whole new level. You can use e-mail at all different stages of customer contact.

THE FIVE BASIC TYPES OF E-MAILS

There are five basic types of e-mails you can send:

1. Awareness- these e-mails let people know about your company and what you have to offer. Generally, these represent the first contact you make with a client.
2. Consideration – these e-mails often compare you to your competitors or highlight specific products and services that you have to offer.
3. Conversion – these e-mails push the hard sell with deals and specific purchase points. These will be the key part of your e-mail marketing strategy.
4. Product usage – these e-mails are sent after a purchase. These include surveys, customer service reminders, delivery confirmations, and product add-ons.
5. Loyalty- these e-mails sustain your relationship to a customer and include such things as product updates, newsletters, events, etc.

E-mail is a great way to give customers information about what you have to offer. But, one of the things any Internet user expects is control over information. Deny your customers this and they will go elsewhere. The Internet lets people browse at their own discretion, and seek only the information, products, and services they most intensely desire. They can easily navigate away from info they don't want, and dump your unopened e-mail into the trash.

Use this to your advantage!

By creating choices for your customers within your online marketing, you give them the empowering ability to select their level of interaction with your brand . . . always, of course, hoping that they will choose increased involvement! Amazon, Netflix, Travelocity, and eBay all allow users to customize what information they get and how often they get it. It's part of what has made these companies such enormous online successes. Below are some suggestions for how to give your customers more control over their relationship with you. They will thank you for it with their loyalty.

WHAT TO SEND

Here's where you need to analyze your own company and figure out what you want to let your clients know about you. Do you have products people can purchase online? Are you a service industry where people can join your service over the Internet (like a bank or insurance company)? Are you a local salon, doctor or restaurant where customers could still learn about what you have to offer at your retail location? All different types of businesses can use e-mail marketing. You just have to know what you want from your e-mail readers. For some useful e-mail templates, you can see examples on our companion website, www.RobertNoll.com

A. The subject line

As a receiver of e-mails, chances are you scan the subject line prior to opening anything. The trick here is to give the recipient a compelling reason to open the e-mail. Let's take the case of an Italian restaurant called Amalfi. An e-mail with the subject line "Amalfi Restaurant News" will receive a lower read rate than an e-mail with the subject line "Amalfi VIP." Because the recipient already e-mail knows who and what Amalfi is, and because everyone loves being called a VIP, this move alone will double, if not triple, your read rate.

Specifics about products, brand names, or events are great words that grab attention in a subject line. Keep your subjects lines to 60 characters or less, and emphasize the benefits to the consumer. Are you offering information? Are you promoting a new product? Can you save them time or money? Pique their curiosity, but be clear about why they should read more.

It's important to avoid using frequent key spam words in your subject lines or e-mails. Avoid mentions of sex or drugs, and be careful when you use words like "instant", "guaranteed", "cash", or "giveaway" unless you also include specific company information.

I recommend always including your company name in your email subject line, and a 3 or 4 word phrase summarizing the specific point of your email: a sale, a coupon, a new product, an article about your industry, etc.

B. The message

Make your message clear and concise. Target the reader with specific tasks: make sure your reader knows what you want them to do (use a coupon, test a new product, come to an event) and how to do it (e-mail you back, check out your website, call in). Save your big stories for a blog, not for e-mail. E-mail has several specific purposes, and once you understand what e-mails are best used for, you will be more able to write useful e-mails.

First, remind your customer who you are. After that, compel them to revisit your business. Third, build a relationship. Always make sure the e-mails are personalized and that you address people by name.

Make clients feel you have read their minds or that you have anticipated their needs and can fulfill them. Use your list software and cookies to personalize and channel e-mails, so that a person looking for camping gear can click through right to your outdoor retail section, whereas a customer looking for scuba gear can get info on the water sports club your store runs.

Use key search terms (not just product names or company-specific terms) in e-mails so readers can search their inboxes for your product. This is true for subject lines and the actual message. Your reader sees at least 40 e-mails a day, sometimes hundreds, so be easy to find!

Another tip is to use mostly text, and don't attach anything! Keep your message simple: either welcome prospective customers to your brand, entice them with specials to make a purchase, or thank them for their purchase and suggest other things they can buy. Keep in mind that people are increasingly reading e-mail on their cell phones or other mobile devices. Simple formats will transfer well, but complicated graphics will not.

Be sure to keep your design consistent along user paths/ between media outlets. Netflix does this well; when you click through their e-mail it opens the site in a cohesive way, so you get right to what you were looking for, instead of having to go all the way through the site. Apple also does this well: they provide, in stores, online, in print and broadcast, a unified multi-media experience. People may also know your brand's look from other media sources—so stay consistent! Your message should be the same no matter how the customer interacts with your company.

WHO TO SEND IT TO

Just as you would do in traditional marketing formats, you have to build a list of leads, or prospective customers. Building your list of leads is easy, and is critical for any business owner. There are some special ways to make sure that the leads you get are viable email addresses and that you are getting email address of anyone who might be interested in your business.

There are several ways to get a list of prospective customers. You want to be more targeted than just e-mailing everyone with an e-mail address, and you want to separate yourself from spammers. One good start is to have an opt-in e-mail list at your point of sale, so you can collect e-mails when people go to your dental office or your restaurant. This way you know you're getting readers who are really interested.

Customers will frequently find your website first. Ask for e-mails on all pages of your website, giving the user multiple entrance points to your e-mail list. Also, on your company website, entice the reader to become a list member. A calendar with in-store events, promotional sweepstakes, and new product testing are all ways to move browsers into subscribers. But make sure you let people choose to be on your list (opt-in), as opposed to just e-mailing anyone who comes to your site. For an example of an ideal opt-in e-mail list sign-up webpage, see Figure 4.1.

Allowing users to opt-in is key, but allowing several options for different types of interaction will allow you to stay in touch even with those not yet in purchasing mode.

Say you have a monthly general newsletter, a weekly special update, and special event promotions. Someone who loves your company and is very interested might want all three types of notifications. Yet you'll still be able to get e-mails out to that prospective or occasional buyer. Catch them at the right time with the right promotion, and, now that you've built their trust in your company, they'll be likely to want more! And remember: people who opt-in to be on e-mail lists purchase 167% more than non-e-mail customers[2].

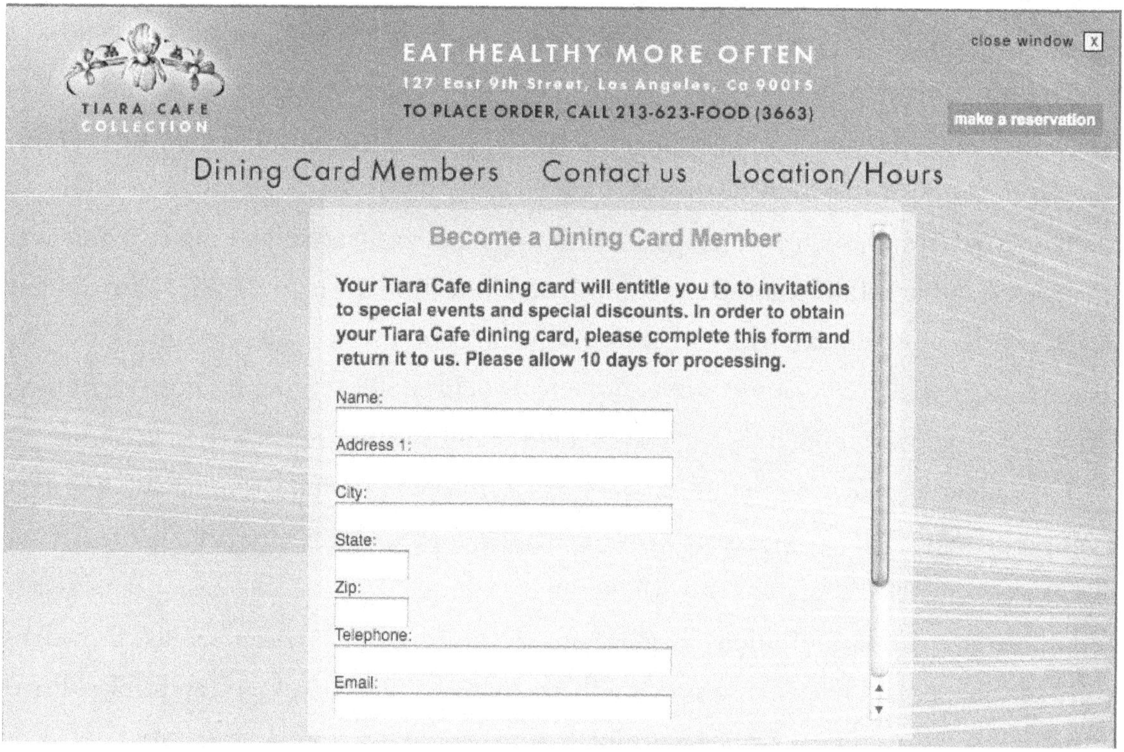

Figure 4.1: Tiara Cafe website

Collect e-mails from a variety of customer contact points, and you are on your way to a huge list of potential clients. But you don't want to send all your emails to all of your customers. Retail clients might not want to hear about your family discount. People who have bought online and shipped out of state might not want your in-store event catalogue if they live overseas. You'll have to balance how much time you can spend emailing people with how much return you get from that investment. If you select who gets what kind of email based on their previous purchases, you'll also show your customers that you pay attention to their needs!

To do this, assign values to these e-mail addresses based on prior purchase history, mailing list information, or type of purchase. Someone who runs their own restaurant and buys flowers from you might be able to fill their restaurant with your flowers, but small families might not be able to invest in such a service.

HOW TO SEND YOUR E-MAILS

Once you start sending out emails to over 100 recipients it's worth it to you to invest a little in an outside email service. Even though your web hosting package probably comes with a variety of e-mail options, I always recommend that Internet marketers e-mail instead use an outside service such as www.icontact.com. Why spend a little money for this? You could find your normal, everyday e-mails barred or banned and marked as spam. It's just not worth the hassle. An outside provider, costing you about $20 a month, may offer you many useful features, such as message scheduling. With this feature you can schedule way in advance and at all different times. Another great feature is Spam Check. This actually analyzes how most inboxes will rate you and your content for spam classifications. The major feature of all e-mail outsource companies is deliverability. Sure, it's not exactly free, but you will get more e-mail through with them than using your own e-mail account.

Companies considering the use of an email marketing program must make sure that their program does not violate spam laws such as the United States' Controlling the Assault of Non-Solicited Pornography and Marketing Act (CAN-SPAM), the European Privacy and Electronic Communications Regulations 2003, or their Internet service provider's acceptable use policy. Even if a company adheres to the applicable laws, it can be blacklisted if Internet e-mail administrators determine that the company is sending spam.

One effective technique used by established e-mail marketing companies is to require what is known as the "double opt-in" method where potential recipients must manually confirm their request for information by clicking a unique link and entering a unique code identifier to confirm that the owner of the recipient e-mail address has indeed requested the information. Responsible e-mail marketing and auto-responder companies use this double opt-in method to confirm each request before any information is sent out.

One great way to make your e-mail stand out in people's inboxes is to time your weekly sending right. E-mail mid-week: inboxes get full on Mondays and Fridays, so hitting them in the middle of the week ups your read rate. Also, since people tend to skim e-mails, give advance time for long-term promotions.

Make it easy for your customers to get the information they want about you, and they will become lifelong customers.

MAINTAINING YOUR E-MAIL CONTACTS

Hitting send is only the beginning of using e-mail marketing as a large-scale strategy. When you start sending out e-mails, or any time you make changes to what you send, take note of who's responding. Evaluate templates in the first three e-mails to find the right mix of link/ logo/ text for you. Find the right size E-mail Service Provider (ESP) and web-analyst for your business. They offer costs and benefits on all sides, but when your list gets large enough and your client needs become more varied, you will need technical expertise to help monitor your online customer activity.

Remember that getting someone to purchase from you is not the end of the story. Aim to maintain the client interaction in a variety of ways. Send people surveys so they can rate your company - people love getting their opinion heard! Make sure to send out confirmations and allow people to track shipping. Transaction e-mails that also market and keep brand awareness give people who have already purchased an easy way to buy similar products/ services, see what other people with similar tastes have bought, and sign up for newsletter/ updates, make product reviews, link to blogs and social sites for reviews, etc. Fed-ex does this well, as do travel sites. When you use e-mail wisely, each interaction can be an opportunity to build customer loyalty, and increase customer interest.

Also, make sure you give clients a way to forward info about your business to others. This kind of virtual word of mouth is one of the best things the Internet has to offer. It's much easier for a runner to send e-mails about shoe specials to her running club than for her to pass out copies of your coupon. Always be on the lookout for ways to expand your online presence.

There are more possibilities to explore with e-mails, much too lengthy to approach here, but the last and most crucial thing is: make it very easy to unsubscribe. Not only does this promote good customer relations, but the law also requires it!

Still not convinced? Whatever you do in life, you're selling something. If you are a business owner, the trick is to "stay ahead of the curve." You will see the day when every business in the U.S., if not worldwide, will collect and market through e-mails. It has been said, "A person who aims at nothing is sure to hit it!" So get moving.

Chapter 5:
Blogging Basics

I USED TO KEEP A journal, as a middle-school kid, and I had to hide it from all of my brothers with intense secrecy. I didn't want anyone who might tease me to read my innermost thoughts. I'd hide it under my bed, deep in my closet, and even lock it to keep it *private*. Years ago, I found on old journal and had a good laugh at what I thought was important as a 12 year old. Now however, as a businessperson looking to get consumers interested in my company, I have started keeping a different kind of journal: a web-log, or blog. It doesn't say who I think is cute, but it does tell people what matters to me, and how I feel about news that affects my industry. And rather than locking it in my closet, I want to share it with *everyone*! If you still think that journals are just for kids, it's time to rethink your business blogging strategy.

We'll teach you what a blog is and how to set one up either through your website or through a parent site. We'll show you how to take a simple online diary and make it a marketing tool for your business. A corporate blog is a frequently overlooked way to promote your business. You will learn how key words and well-crafted topics will easily attract business for free. When you have a blog that lets customers leave comments, it's like being a fly on the wall, in the sense that you can hear what people have to say about your business, product, or service, and you can respond accordingly.

When you set up a blog, you have lots of options to consider before you even write your first post. First there are publishing options, then author options, then topic options, and finally overall blog structure options. So many options! We'll help you evaluate what choices will be right for *your* business blog.

PUBLISHING YOUR BLOG

There are a number of different ways you can publish information online, and which method you chose depends on how much time you have to invest, how tech-savvy you are, and what you want your blog to accomplish for your company. Blogs can be hosted by dedicated blog hosting services, or they can be run using blog software, or on regular web hosting services. There are plusses and minuses for all of these options.

A. Dedicated Blog Hosting Services

Blogging sites such as Live Journal, Blogspot, and the blogs on MySpace are a bit too generic for the business wanting to create a specific user experience. However, these are great sites for beginner bloggers who want to start publishing and want an easy, low maintenance blog with a pre-existing network structure. Since thousands of bloggers and readers are connected on these sites for personal and professional reasons, these sites can offer community in a variety of ways. If you agree to it, they can list your blog on other related blogs, or make it very easy for other people to check out your blog.

Figure 5.1: www.Livejournal.com homepage

Blogging sites also tend to require less technical programming knowledge, so if you want to post a simple text entry and one photo, and you only want to work on your blog for an hour every week, this is a great way to accomplish it. Also, if you want to set up a basic layout and then forget about it, or if you want all the administrative duties to be automatically done for you, these sites are for you.

Figure 5.2: www.blogspot.com example

On the other hand, if you are looking for a more personalized Web experience for your readers, or to control more of the blog functions or measurements, and you have some interest in building your programming skills, try one of these other hosting options.

B. Blog Software

A great way to make a blog individualized is by using a program such as Word Press or Typepad to publish it. You can download these software programs onto your computer and modify the look of your blog. These highly malleable software programs allow you to do numerous things such as update your blog frequently, add lots of media elements, truncate posts, segment your blog into multiple topic subheadings, allow different authors, and more. You will have to do a little work in setting up your blog, but the effort can pay off in the long run if you want to make your blog a big part of your business site.

Wordpress allows very personalized blogs, best if you offer services that are constantly changing, or if your industry serves a strong online demographic. A car repair shop can make do with a simpler blog, updated by staff about anything from special deals and new services, to personal interest stories. However, an online legal consulting firm might want a Twitter feed, RSS feed, and blog network since it does a large portion of its business on line, for clients who are online, about a constantly evolving industry.

Some people have made their blogs their business, such as Seth Godin. He writes Seth's Blog, and his use of Typepad makes it easy for readers to search his own blog, search Google, look at archived entries, and subscribe to the blog and e-mail lists.

DON'T MISS A THING
FREE UPDATES BY EMAIL

Enter your email address

me@email.com

Subscribe me!   preview

powered by FeedBlitz

RSS FEEDS

SUBSCRIBE
BOOKMARK
By Twitter: @thisissethablog

SEARCH

Google™

search

○ WWW   ● SETH'S BLOG

Email Me

SETH'S WEB PAGES

The Dip Blog

newspapers—they have a churn and burn mentality. The internet turns this upside down. The internet is about who, not how many. The internet lets you take really good care of 100 people instead of harassing 2,000.

Yet, panicked marketers still look for scale (How many followers can we get? What can we do with a Facebook fan page?) and then hijack that attention, hoping to filter out the masses and get a few sales.

Scalejacking inevitably tarnishes most communities, because individuals (people) hate being treated like numbers just standing by to be filtered.

Stephen Stills wrote, "If you can't be with the one you love, love the one you're with." I think he was wrong. On the Internet, the mantra that works is, "Be with the ones you love (and the ones that love you.)" Ignore everyone else. It doesn't have good internal pentameter, but it's true.

Technorati Links • Save to del.icio.us (16 saves, tagged: marketing sethgodin socialmedia) • Digg This! (7 Diggs, 2 comments) • Email this • Stumble It! • Subscribe to this feed • Share on Facebook • Twit This!

Posted by Seth Godin on June 17, 2009 | Permalink | TrackBack (0)

What's off the table?

No project is conceived in a vacuum, no decision in isolation and no negotiation with a clean sheet of paper.

But do you know what you're *not* willing to consider?

If a newspaper company is planning its future, is shutting down the printing presses an option even being considered? Or is it off the table?

Plan a rabbi's wedding and you probably shouldn't even bother to pitch BLT sandwiches or lobster. It's off the table. Not being considered.

Figure 5.3: Seth's blog at http://sethgodin.typepad.com

C. Regular Web Hosting Services

Hosting your blog on your own website means that you need to have hired a good programmer or that you are good at programming and updating your website. If you want your blog to be highly personalized and to look a very particular way, using your own webpage as a blog can make the user experience more cohesive. But pretty much everyone who is not a computer whiz should think about letting someone else do the legwork. You will have to know how to alter the Java script or HTML code of your website to update each entry, and if you want to post videos or photos or podcasts, you will have to work a little harder. But there are some very dynamic, eye catching blogs out there, and if you want to dedicate to the time, and if you have the server space on your website, then hosting the blog on your own page can really make it stand out.

Who should write your blog?

Now you need to evaluate what you want your blog to say, which will dictate who says it. The whole purpose of a corporate blog is to let your consumers and potential consumers know more about your company. When people read your blog, they should feel like they have inside information about your company and your industry that the average shopper lacks. So, consider who might want to read your blog, and what they might want to know about your company. Do they want tutorials on how to use your products? Do they want the latest research on your industry? Do they want to know more about your company and what makes it tick? Answering these questions is a key step in determining the direction of your blog. From there, you will need to consider if you want to be the main blog voice, or if you want to allow other employees to share their input.

If you have a great way with words, or loads of time to stay up to date on your industry, then you might want to be the sole author of your business blog. As the sole blogger, you are responsible for moderating all comments, creating post topics, linking and networking your site, managing the layout and media uploads, tracking readership – as you can see, it can be a big endeavor. But if you run a small business (just you?) or if you want total control over your material, or if you are the company expert and the rest of your staff is mostly technicians, you might be the best blog author.

But maybe you want to personalize your company by letting the employees share what they love about working there, or how they like to use your company's product.

So, if you work at a small theatre company with staff of actors, designers, playwrights, crew technicians, etc, you might want them all to contribute a post so that patrons get a broader understanding of your company.

What to write about

The people who read your blog will have a wide range of experience and information about your company, from people who use your service frequently to experts in your field to people who stumbled upon your site with little background in what you do. So you need to have a few plans of attack here; you need to decide how much of an insider blog you want to create. Is your blog accessible to the everyday reader, or is it full of technical jargon that only an industry insider would understand?

Creating topics for your blog depends on your overall strategy and on who gives input in to your blog. Your readers might want to know more about:

o New products and services
o Changes to old products and services
o Testimonials from users
o Store Events/ promotions
o Relevant articles on your industry
o Interviews with industry experts
o Changes to company leadership/ major staff
o Relevant staff information

Once you start posting regularly and getting comments, the direction of your blog will become clear as people comment on what they find important. Always be willing to open your blog up to what your customers would want to hear. Whatever you post, make it topical, professional, and approachable. It should be personal enough that readers feel invited into your company. So, if you have a staff member retiring who has been a long time part of your office, announce it on a blog! Make consumers feel connected to you and they will reward you with customer loyalty!

Remember the art and selling power of *the story*: Your Story. Readers want more than just a laundry list of company products. In addition to specifics and promotions and events, make sure to give some insight into your business, what makes you special, what inspired you to go into your line of work, and why you are passionate about what you do.

Maybe you have interns who are following your company with an eager eye to learn the business, maybe you have a specific events/ community outreach person, maybe you have a marketing director, or maybe you wear all these hats at once! If the tone of your blog is relatively consistent, your blog will be more appealing. A mix of outside expert articles, and business-specific inside tips will give your blog the balance of accessibility and expertise that you need to attract readers and keep them tuning back in.

You'll need to increase your industry literacy in order to make your blog up to date. Find the relevant blogs to your industry and check them frequently. You'll also be commenting on these sites and seeking tag backs from the other bloggers. Remember, the Internet is here to work for you. Cast your net wide, and then be picky about what you select to focus on.

Update regularly, and seek out related articles about your industry. Are you a travel agent and China is having a big festival season coming up? Are you a bookstore offering a new work by an author featured in a national bestseller list? Do you know new health care research that your patients will want to know? It just takes a few minutes each week, or a few posts a month, to keep your blog an active part of your company's marketing strategy.

Transmitting vs. Engaging with your readers

Online networks practically demand that you go above and beyond just transmitting information to consumers in a static way. Consumers want to feel involved in your company, and if you give them the chance to input and participate, not only will they give you clear feedback, they'll be more likely to pass you on. Blogs are a great way to transmit information, but they are also a great way to involve the reader.

Try offering contests, requesting feedback, and seeking out funny new uses for products or testimonials from your consumers (How was the trip they took with you? Do they have a great new recipe using your cutting board?).

Make your blog interactive; interactivity is what the Web is all about. If customers feel engaged in your company, they'll feel invested in returning. Ask for comments and reviews, and remind people to share your site by e-mailing links, images and video and event invitations.

Blogs are also a great place to advertise with coupons and special offers. You know the people who read your blog are interested in what you have to offer, so reward your followers with special blog only promotions.

Include calls to action even on your blog. If you post an article about mold in houses for your carpet installation company, make sure the blog emphasizes the need for customers to get their carpets redone - by you!

Teaching is another great way to make your site more interactive. Teach a class online once a month or a few times a year: if you own a car repair shop, teach people how to change a tire, check their oil, do small repairs, or diagnostics so they know when to come in to you for larger services.

For more tips on what to add to your blog and how to get it off the ground, check out our website, www.RobertNoll.com. We can lead you step by step through all the stages of creating your blog, and give you hints about what to include in your posts.

Make sure people know that you want your blog link spread around. If you are hosting your own blog, make your blog posts individual pages so they are easier to send as links, directing people right where they want to go. Remember, online, consumers expect to control the user experience, so when you give them some control, you get their respect … and their return business.

Handling comments

Make sure you have a comment filter to filter out spam or obscenities on your blog. Other related companies will track down your blog, and often there is an unspoken agreement between blogs to return comments on a blog if someone comments on yours and you want to build a relationship.

You can and should moderate posts to your blog when possible. The host you use will dictate how much control you have over what people post to your site. Post moderation requires users to register before commenting, or requires individual posts or comments to be approved by a moderator or administrator before they appear in the blog. Weblog applications use various user account systems that allow readers to post comments to a particular blog. For instance, users with Blogger accounts may comment on any Blogger blog. Other weblog applications allow users to post content or comments only to blogs where they have an account.

But a word about comments: view these as an opportunity to interact and engage with your readers and customers, and a way to network with other bloggers. Don't be afraid of negative comments, and certainly don't eliminate them or sweep them under the virtual rug. A prompt, direct, respectful response to a negative comment can establish a reputation for great customer service. If at all possible, since blog comments can instantly be public, encourage people to call you with complaints so you can deal with them personally. Otherwise, one displeased customer can stain your blog forever.

NETWORKING WITH OTHER BLOGGERS

Once you have your own blog established, get out there and get involved in reading and posting on related industry blogs. Not only should your company website should have a blog, and you should have a career focused blog for yourself that directly relates to your company. Then start looking around for other blogs about your industry, starting with the national company blogs. Some CEOs are even writing blogs, so check them out. Then look at whom they link to, and who comments on them. By doing a little blog research, you can see what other people believe is relevant to your industry.

When you find well written and popular blogs related to your industry, try commenting on other blogs in a debate format. Opening a dialogue with other industry bloggers is a great way to expand your readership. For a great business marketing blog, check out www.wilsonweb.com, and take a look at the multiple facets of his blog.

· Install an "e-mail this post" feature on your blog so that people can easily forward your articles on to friends. The easier you make it for people to share your blog, the more you expand your readership! You can set a lot of these extra sharing functions in the setting section of your blog, so that they can be translated in a wide range of languages, get added to the blog directories, and any other site updating list that your host offers. This is one of the benefits of using a larger Web service to post your blog.

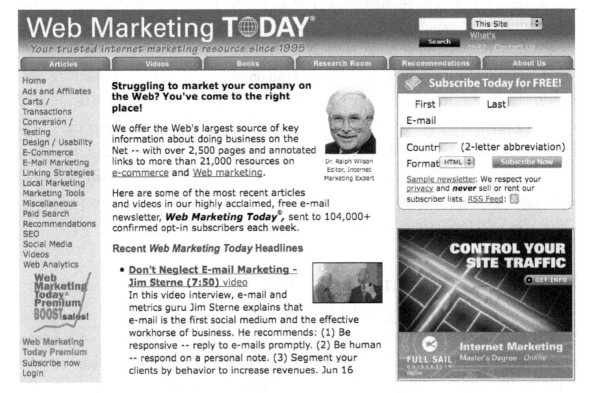

Figure 5.4: www.wilsonweb.com

Link to other blogs. Links are the currency of the blogosphere and it takes money to make money, so start linking. Technorati, Blogscope, and Bloglines are all search sites for blogs where people will look for your blog. Register on these sites, and interested parties will be able to find you.

Install a blogroll. It's a very simple yet effective social networking scheme and it has the same result as a simple link if not stronger: traffic! So if you don't have one yet, sign up for a blogroll and get that link list going.

Be an active commenter. This is in the same vein as linking. Most comment systems also provide a way for you to leave a link back to your blog, which begs a visit at the very least. So if you feel inspired, leave a comment or two in your blog travels. It behooves you to expand your blog network.

Bloggers are constantly trying to network and connect with other bloggers. One way to expand your blogosphere is to read blogs of other related industry professionals and then reference their entries in your own blog. When you do this, you should send a trackback, linking their site to yours. A trackback is a ping (little message) that is sent to a website letting them know that you've referenced their entry in an entry of your own. Some websites show trackbacks with a link to your site "inline" with their entry. Diggers Realm does this and displays everyone who trackbacks under the story. Most blogs have a list of how many trackbacks a particular entry has received, showing how much influence that blog entry has.

You can use your blogging platform to automatically send out PINGS to any other webpage you mentioned in your entry, and blogging etiquette demands that the cited authors link to your article.

Make sure you link to a relevant article. Avoid being SPING: pings that are merely spam. Remember that being known as a trusted source of info is the best way to build an online following. There are even spam filters on trackbacks that will check the origin of your post to make sure that you are a legitimate blog.

MONITORING YOUR BLOG

Keep track of your company's marketing progress with analytics for your blog. There are many ways to see who is reading your blog and how they found it, and how frequently they come back. Comments themselves are a great way to keep track of who is reading your blog, but there are probably far more "lurkers" and casual readers that you could engage more actively. Google offers Feedburner for blogger users, and Wordpress and Type pad all offer their own analytics, so you can see how many people are subscribed to your feeds, where your Web content is being re-syndicated, and whether your revenue per subscriber is equal to your revenue per unique visitor on your website.

BLOG SEARCH ENGINES

Use blog search engines to find your competition and see what they are writing about. Submit your address to blog search sites and directories. People look for blog content at

Technorati every day, are you on their list? You should be. Submit your blog's URL to Technorati, Daypop, Blogdex, Popdex, and any other site of that ilk you come across.

Keep search engines in mind. There are a few things you can do to make your blog more search engine friendly. For example, use post titles and post page archiving. This will automatically give each of your post pages an intelligent name based on the title of your post. Also, try to be descriptive when you blog. A well-crafted post about something very specific can end up very near the top results of a search.

Keep your posts and paragraphs short. Strive for succinct posts that pump pertinent new information into the blogosphere and move on. Keep it short and sweet so visitors can pop in, read up, and click on.

AVOIDING BLOG SPAM

Avoid turning your blog into a Spam Blog. Spam sites can create robots that will fill your blog with spam comments. To avoid this, make commenters verify their e-mail addresses. This not only eliminates the possibility for spammers to overload and advertise on your site, but it also offers another place for your customers to give their information to you. Also, once people have committed to commenting in your blog, they will be reassured that you are not a spam site when you send them a confirmation e-mail with an opt-in option for future updates, e-mail coupons, special deals, etc.

THE FUTURE OF BLOGGING

As the news moves increasingly online, "legitimacy" and "community" are going to be the two big buzzwords of online publishing. Establishing yourself as an expert or a reputable source can make you stand out. By affiliating your blog with other important national sites, and by listing your credentials (and linking to the certifying boards), your blog will become a go-to place for news about your industry.

Also, the more you link your blog to social media (in the next few chapters), the more people will pass your blog around. In fact, some see the future of small business blogging as creating collectives or co-ops of similar industry blogs so that smaller businesses can share readership. We'll see who will agree to that.

The real moral of the blogging story is that if you put a reliable, up-to-date, interesting and relevant blog out to your customers, the odds are good that they will keep checking up on what you have to say. Be consistent and professional, and the readers will follow.

Next, we'll show you how to extend your blogosphere by allowing readers to subscribe to your blog, keeping them updated on everything new going on at your company.

Chapter 6:
Feeds

EXTRA! EXTRA! READ ALL ABOUT it! You do want everyone to read your blog, right? Well, if you're like me and you read several blogs regularly, and you follow the news on CNN. com, AND you like to check in with a few other national publications online, AND you have a blog of your own. It can be dizzying to chase down all that information online. Imagine you had to personally walk around to all the different news sources you were interested in, and pick up the hard news from them. You'd end up carrying around a lot of articles you were not very likely to read, and you might not get to all the sources in one day. Plus, you would need new shoes all the time! Feeds keep you from having to hoof it around the Internet and sift through long blog updates. They help collect all the news you want in one convenient place, and give you a brief subject line and blurb about what each article is about. Sounds helpful, doesn't it? Now, you wouldn't want to be one of the sources that people couldn't walk around to in a day, right? In that case, you need to help your readers out by allowing them to subscribe to your blog on a feed.

Now that you have the basics of blogging down, it's time to increase your readership, the number of people who regularly check your blog. One easy way to turn your homegrown blog into an internationally followed publication (Hey, why not dream big!) is to allow readers to subscribe to a news feed of your posts. Back in the early days of the Internet, if you liked a website and wanted to see the updates on that website, you would bookmark it. Then you would have to continually go back to that bookmark and check up on the page, and to do this for each site you liked. Bookmarking didn't let you know when a page had been updated, so the onus was totally on you to seek out a page each time you thought about it.

Feeds streamline the process by collecting all the sites you find interesting into one page, and automatically updating their entries for you. It's an easy way to keep readers informed. Instead of hoping that people check your blog regularly by going to your website, they'll be instantly alerted to new posts or other updates as they scroll through their other valued news. Also, feeds save you some of the PR work of e-mailing readers each time you post something on your blog. Now, your post will be right next to CNN's latest news on a personalized aggregator page for each customer. Your subscribers can read updates on all the news they want, from their favorite cartoon to the latest movie reviews, from international news headlines to financial updates, all along with *your company's news*, in the same convenient location.

In this chapter we will describe how feeds work, the different methods of subscription, what to post on an aggregator site, how to attract readers to subscribe to your feed, and how to keep them engaged with your company's posts. For extensive examples of good and bad blogs, as well as other ways to encourage readers to subscribe to you, see the latest in the blog section of the companion website, www.RobertNoll.com.

HOW FEEDS WORK

A site feed is a computer readable representation of your blog that can be picked up and displayed on other websites and information aggregation tools. For other people to easily read entries from your blog, they might subscribe to your site through software that searches your blog for updates, then aggregates the new entries with other new entries. It's a bit like having a constant news scrawl available to you, collecting news stories from a wide range of sources. One great thing about feeds is that you can disseminate your stories instantly to anyone who wants to follow your blog.

Blogs and news sites can all be syndicated because they get updated on a regular basis, unlike static websites. Once someone has subscribed to your blog on their feed reader (more on these in a second), their site will instantly be notified of any updates to your site, and they will see all or part of your new post when they check their feed reader.

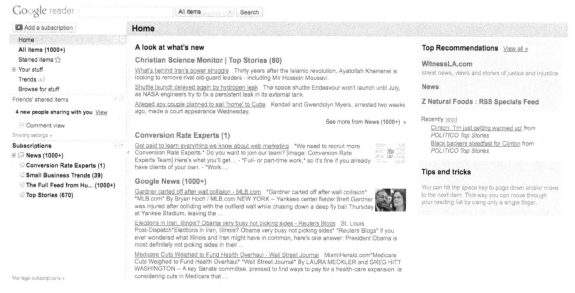

Figure 6.1: Google.com feed reader

1. Feed readers

What is a feed reader? Well, it's a website, such as Google Reader or Mybloglog, where users collect sites that they want to follow (See Figure 6.1). Users get accounts on these sites- most e-mail servers allow this as well- and then when they subscribe to your blog using a feed reader, they no longer have to return to your website. Feed reader websites have software that, like search engines, scrolls the selected pages online for updates and sends those updates back to the reader's site. Then, the posts all get aggregated into the feed reader, creating an online personal newspaper!

Google and Yahoo! both offer feed readers that aggregate news stories and blog entries from sites that you can select to see on your homepage. That way, you can surf information you want from one portal. If you create interesting, relevant blog content, update your blog consistently, and make it easy for people to add your blog to their feeds, you'll be able to reach readers quickly and efficiently.

However you host your blog (your own website or an outside platform like Wordpress or blogger), you can turn on syndication in the blog settings. You can either opt to share full stories of your blog or short log lines to let people know that you have updated. Depending on how brief your message is, and how dedicated your followers are, choose how much you want people to see in their feeds. You can also choose to allow the feeds to show comments or not. So, if your commentators tend to be informative and positive, this is a great way to build your blogging network. Professional bloggers like Seth Godin or Scott Adams know how to do this, and recognize the importance of building a loyal fan base.

2. Syndication services

RSS and ATOM are the two different main types of syndication—some sites use one or both in their aggregators. The best bet is to enable your blog for both models of syndication, to make sure you can attract the widest audience.

When you enable RSS feeds on your blog, the RSS symbol will show up in the browser where your URL is. You can also include other RSS buttons on your blog, depending on how you host your site (See Figure 6.2 below). For instance, your readers might want to subscribe to your blog so they see it on their own blog site, or on their social media site, or on their e-mail homepage. The more options you give people to follow you, the more likely they will be to do so.

Also, you can post a feed footer at the bottom of all your feeds (with your company website link!) to keep your info very visible and accessible. The more easily people can follow a clear trail from information they find interesting about you to your company homepage, the closer you come to having a customer!

WHAT TO POST FOR FEEDS

Blogs and newsletters, relevant articles, current videos: if it's on your website or blog and it's news, post it! A feed keeps your customers updated, so if there's new information, put it up there, and do it in any medium you can. The wider range of media you use, the better. Got a new product? Post a blog announcing it, then a relating article about the new technology, then some user reviews, then some photos or videos of people interacting with the product. Become your own press agent. Feeds are best for those frequently updated blogs, so if you only look at your blog once every couple of months, readers won't respond to your feed. But if you keep updating with fresh, relevant content, your subscriber base will grow, and you'll reach more and more possible customers.

Figure 6.2: Feed syndication button on www.Dilbert.com

If you have a website, blog, audio/video content, or even photos, you can offer a feed of your content as an option. If you are using a popular blogging platform or publishing tool like TypePad, Wordpress, or Blogger, you likely publish a feed automatically. Even other non-blogging sites like social photo-sharing service Flickr offer feeds of content you produce that others can retrieve. There are also tools on the market that can help transform traditional Web content into the right format for distribution.

HOW TO ATTRACT SUBSCRIBERS

The first and most obvious way to attract subscribers is to be a good blogger! This means updating frequently (at least a few times a week), with relevant, interesting, well-written content. If your blog sits around and you post something to it only when you have free time, no one will follow you. Imagine if the L.A. Times only issues papers once in a while. How many subscribers do you think they would retain? Also check out Chapter 5 for more on blogging.

Once you have a steady stream of interesting, relevant content, you need to link up with your readers. Consider posting a blog roll on the side of your blog site. A blog roll unites your blog with other readers, like an RSS feed in reverse. This application lets people who read your blog see who else reads your blog and which blogs you subscribe to. Much like the Amazon recommendation system, if people like what you have to say, they are more likely to check out other like-minded publications.

Another great way blogs attract subscribers is by networking with other bloggers. See which blogs pop up in a search of your field, and take a look at who is reading them. Post on their blogs with comments, and in your comment make sure people can easily link back to your site, read what fascinating stuff you have to say, and subscribe to you!

Also, check out forums and groups for your target demographics and put in a comment on the group discussion boards, then include a link to your site. Anywhere you go on the Web, look for ways to invite people to subscribe to your feed.

HOW TO KEEP SUBSCRIBERS

If you want to keep your readers subscribed, update, update, update! When your content is fresh, interesting, and relevant to your readers, they will be more likely to subscribe to your feed. If you don't have new stuff to say, no one will want to follow you. In addition to the tips you learned in Chapter 5, here are some great blog post ideas from some small business bloggers.

Most blogging software allows you to see how many subscribers you have in addition to how many page views you have. You can even post that ticker on your blog, so if your blog becomes popular, you can brag, and invite people to join the legions of subscribers. But, at first, keep this info to yourself, and give some time for your blog to gain momentum and for you to master your personal blogging style.

If you really want you can spend a little extra money to get highly specific feedback about who's following your blog and how they got there. Google offers Feedburner, their blog analytics system, so you can see how many people are subscribed to your feeds, where your Web content is being re-syndicated, and whether your revenue per subscriber is equal to your revenue per unique visitor on your website.

FeedBurner's services allow publishers who already have a feed to improve their understanding of and relationship with their audience. Once you have a working feed, run it through FeedBurner and realize a whole new set of benefits.

RSS feeds are an important factor in increasing blog readership since they are part of increasing interactivity on your site and putting your company smack in the center of the online community. RSS feeds automatically bring updated information straight to the desktop of subscribers. Users can monitor news, blogs and more. An increasing number of websites offer RSS feeds, identified by a small button denoting either RSS or XML. Enabling your site with an RSS component allows audiences to subscribe to your company's news and information as well as pass it along to other interested parties, generating conversation and interest along the way.

OTHER AGGREGATE SITE OPTIONS

There is a range of sites that are like feeds in that they aggregate stories that other people find interesting. Digg, Del.i.cious, Stumbleupon, and Reddit are all examples of sites where Web surfers post things they find interesting online. Our companion website, found at the end of this book with your special access code, will link you to all these sites in one convenient location!

When Web surfers visit your site or your blog, and they find what you have posted interesting and important enough to spread around, not only can they e-mail it to other people, link to it on their own site, subscribe to it, and comment on it, they can also post it to one of these aggregator sites!

There are two basic ways to get involved on these sites:

1. Start browsing them and checking out which ones are right for your business, which of these sites might have appropriate material for the types of posts you want to make. Make comments on the posts related to your industry, and include links back to your site in your post, along with your site URL. If you leave insightful, well written comments, the people who read that post will be able to bounce back to your site. You might have gained a subscriber and, more importantly, a customer!

2. The other way to get involved on these aggregator sites is to make it very easy on your blog for people to forward your posts on to these sites. Have the icons for your top sites easily clickable both in a general navigation bar on your blog homepage, and in each post. All blogging software can help you customize these options. Activate your blog for PINGING with all the major search sites (Google, Yahoo!, MSN) so people will quickly know that you have updated it. With all the search crawlers out there, you want your info to get out quickly to the masses!

Make your information easy to spread and people will be more likely to spread it!

SECTION 3:

SOCIAL MEDIA

I BET YOU THOUGHT FRIENDS were people you knew well, or who you saw on a regular basis. Friends were people who grew up with you. Or maybe you thought that you had to lose touch with some friends when you moved apart. Not anymore! The Internet has changed the meaning of the word "friend," and has completely revolutionized how people stay in contact with each other.

Welcome to Web 2.0, where the consumers of today and tomorrow gather information from names and faces they recognize. Whereas the Internet used to be seen as a relatively static tool for information gathering, Web 2.0 envisions the Internet as a global community, where everyone is connected and can share information with each other. Once your company starts to market itself as a member of this interactive global network, you'll target potential consumers, who will freely share information about you to their networks, who will pass it on to others . . . The dream of online marketers!

Social networking is the wave of the future. Some online professionals have even said that Search Engines are dead! Using social networking sites you can establish, promote, discuss, market, and advertise your company for free. You can also contact people that match your target demographic for free.

In the global economy, you can now network with like-minded companies and potential consumers from all over the world. You can learn more about your repeat customers and your business contacts from search engine background checks than you could ever learn over cocktail hour. With social marketing websites, your web of networking can extend far beyond that of your handshake! So make your contacts count.

SECTION 3: SOCIAL MEDIA

In the next few chapters, we will discuss in detail the pros, cons, and dangers of various social networks. Depending on your business type, social networking can look unprofessional. We'll discuss which types of companies would benefit most from which social media sites and which types of companies should avoid social marketing entirely.

Chapter 7:
Business-to-Business Networking

A FEW MONTHS AGO, MY university had a happy hour event for alums living in my city. I went, looking forward to seeing some old friends and meeting a few new faces. The event was enjoyable, including the few speakers and the speed-networking format. I was able to make some great new contacts and touch base with a few people I have been wanting to work with, but haven't had a chance to seek out. However, I was really sad to see that quite a few friends that I knew lived in town weren't present.

I bet you've had a similar experience. Missed opportunities are everywhere, and it's up to you to try and stop missing them! Sure, face-to-face networking is invaluable, but sometimes it isn't possible. Luckily, there are ways to connect with peers and colleagues online that can help you extend your business network, without endless rounds of cocktails and old war stories.

As an online marketer, Web 2.0 is a term you have to know. This is the next stage of the Internet that is blossoming right now. In the old days, the Internet was used as an information portal, but no longer. Today's Web isn't just static pages and limited interaction. Now the Internet facilitates relationships, engaging users in a variety of ways. We can move information and connect people globally! The democratic, personal, do-it-yourself components of the Web let people integrate their favorite websites into their lives.

The goal of business social networking sites is to seek out contacts in a direct, aggressive manner. You can go right to people and ask if they want to know more about your company or not. Allowing the users the choice of how much to interact with you actually makes them more likely to interact with you! These contacts, or "friends", will lead you to more friends, and these friends will interact with you the more you interact with them.

Social Media takes constant diligence. You will want to go on to your profile page at least once a day to see who is asking to add you as a friend, to find new friends, to comment on other blogs and profiles, and to monitor the comments people are leaving on your profile. There is a comment log on your page, where anyone can post comments about you on your profile where everyone can see them. Inevitably, you will get some negative comments, or some inappropriate comments, or some spam from companies trying to sell you stuff. Luckily, you can eliminate these comments. With real comments, you will want to respond ASAP, and with spam or junk, you will have to erase them. If you have time, you can filter all your comments for approval before you post, which is a really great idea—it gives you more control over what is publicly visible, such as negative comments from customers or unprofessional posts from your personal friends.

Let consumers feel like they have discovered you! Make your messages personal to them.

As of 2009, 71% of the US population is online, all ages and classes.[1] However, not every online marketing platform may be appropriate for your business. For example, would your dental office benefit from using Friendster or Google Maps, or both? In this case, a Friendster profile might make your office seem unprofessional, whereas appearing on a Google Maps search legitimizes your company. However, if you own an online clothing store, it would be advantageous to advertise on Friendster because creating a social community will help you contact prospective buyers and connect them to your brand in a more personal way. But what if you want your company to operate with more professionalism, yet you still want to connect with other industry insiders and with potential customers online?

MySpace, Friendster, Facebook are all great sites if your target demographic is really skewed young. But if you run an insurance agency or hospital equipment company, you can still establish a trustworthy, respectable social media presence if you go to the right places. On sites like LinkedIn and Ryze, you can find, be introduced to, refer, and collaborate with qualified professionals that you need to work with to accomplish your goals. Social Marketing can help you create a network of contractors and business contacts with whom you might have lost touch. Though these social networks are not as great for marketing directly to clients, they are a great way to promote your company to possible vendors, contractors, and business affiliates.

FIND THE RIGHT B2B NETWORK FOR YOU

As social media becomes an increasingly important part of corporate networking, it stands to reason that there are a growing number of business-to-business networking sites. Each of these has a slightly different target group, and different feature that may or may not be helpful to your company. Also, when joining a social network site, consider how useful it is to your specific industry. Are the members largely tech companies, service industries, small businesses? Since the purpose of business to business networks are to connect you to companies that are relevant to your industry, only join those sites where you might find useful contacts.

LinkedIn

LinkedIn.com is the key networking site for all businesspeople to join. The first big social business network, LinkedIn has over 36 million members in over 200 countries and territories around the world. And don't think that only small business owners are testing the social network waters. Executives from all Fortune 500 companies are LinkedIn members. So, if you make the right connections, you could wind up with some big industry players in your network! Search through the list of people and companies and make sure you are on LinkedIn.com

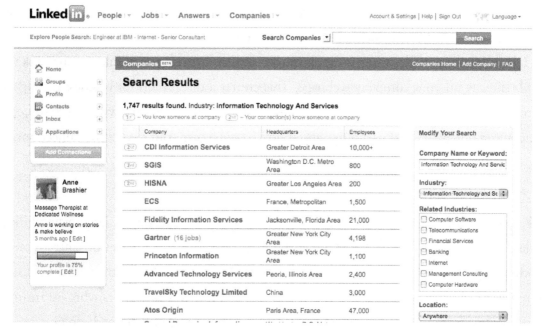

Figure 7.1: www.LinkedIn.com

On all of these business networking sites, as on social media sites, the more public information you provide in a convenient location, the easier it is for people to find you! So, make sure on each site that you include your website, hours, location, detailed description, links to press, and any other relevant information. Also, play around on these sites- they all offer unique features that can set you apart from your competition. For instance, on LinkedIn, you can give fill out the Q&A section, allowing people to see your opinions on hot topics in your field. Setting up your personal and company profiles are like building your business card- use your website as a good model. If it's on your website, include it on your LinkedIn page!

On LinkedIn, you will make connections with people you know or want to know more who are related to you in some way. These can be former coworkers, friends of present co-workers, or new business contacts with whom you want to establish a stronger relationship. When you first set up an account, both a personal account and a company profile, you will then seek out connections.

One nice component of LinkedIn is that it instantly scans your webmail server for contacts using LinkedIn, so you can easily invite them to be part of your network. The feature also scans for duplicate e-mails and changed e-mail addresses so that you can get the most current contact information for these people.

LinkedIn also provides widgets (applications) so that you can put a link to your LinkedIn profile directly on your company webpage. This creates a direct path for business contacts to become business comrades! Connect to LinkedIn through our website at www.RobertNoll.com, and you can find all sorts of useful tips about how to maximize your LinkedIn connections.

RYZE

RYZE.com is a similar site for small business owners. Though not as large a network as LinkedIn, this site still offers great networking services. Since it focuses on entrepreneurs looking to grow their businesses, this site tends to be even less social than LinkedIn, and more assertively business focused. This is best for small business owners who are running their own businesses. If you are your sole employee and your service depends on networking with other services, RYZE.com might be a good site for you to get on. For instance, if you are a make-up artist looking to work with wedding photographers, you can link with those professionals on RYZE.

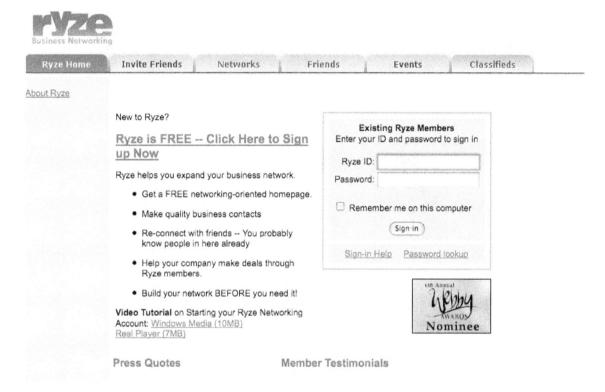

Figure 7.2: www.Ryze.com

Tribe.net

Tribe.net is another business networking site with a bit less formal approach. It's a great place for artists and cultural institutions, art galleries, designers, etc. to network. But remember: these networking sites are all only as good as the connections that are on them with you. When a site stops adding connections, or when its network stagnates, it might be time to pack up and more to a more crowded location.

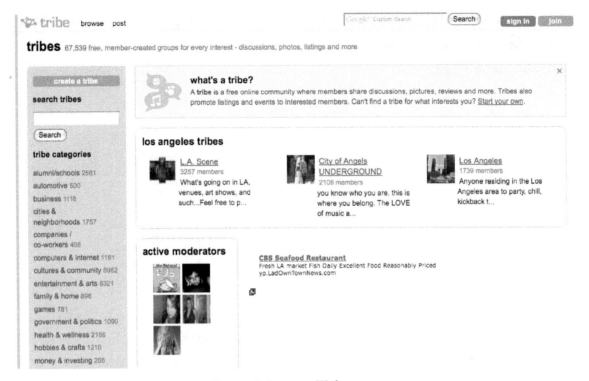

Figure 7.3: www.Tribe.com

Industry-Specific Networking Sites

Niche markets for specific industries are a great way to find out what the competition is up to, create affiliations between related industries, share new industry developments, and arrange larger events. Seek them out through searches, ask around at conferences, or make your own!

If you go on Ning.com, a site that provides tools so anyone can create a niche social network, you can find all sorts of narrow professional networks. However, some of them don't have much of a membership yet. But if you have a prominent place in your industry you can spread the news and invite people to join.

Industry specific networking sites also have stricter authentication standards than other social sites to make sure that you are who you say you are. For example, Sermo. com, a medical professional network, authenticates each of its members by checking their credentials against several of the 10,000 databases they have access to. The service also requires users to answer three verifiable personal questions, ranging from their phone number to where they got their medical degrees before they can sign up.

The tech professional network INmobile.org relies on member referrals and e-mail confirmations, but says it is looking into stricter methods, like calling up the person or their colleagues, since e-mails can be easily faked. The service says it turns away more than half who apply, admitting only director-level employees and above from large companies, top-level executives from smaller companies and vice-president level and above from midsize businesses.

The social network world is constantly changing, so test out a number of sites. Chances are good that if you can find a lot of your contacts in the network already, it's a valuable site for you to join.

HOW TO USE B2B NETWORKING

With social marketing, it's easy to assume that the community will automatically get involved with you via your profile(s), network of friends, content submission, voting and participation. That's the big mistake most marketers make when trying to promote products and services on the social Web. They'll create an account on a social media site, put up some content and expect the social media world to be their oyster without having built a network first.

Once you have an account, publicize it! A post about your new network profile on your blog can let your followers know that there is a new way to connect to you. On your contact page of your website, let people join your social network. Most of these sites have a widget, or an API, that allows you to embed a logo button on your own page, which instantly connects the user to the corresponding website.

Also, in person, make sure your business card has your website and e-mail address, and invite people you meet face to face to become your friends or connections on social networking sites. That way you move from immediate contacts to global contacts!

Make sure you calculate the trade off that the time being fully connected in a social network requires. Participating fully in social media as a business and marketing strategy requires discipline, some tech research, and a daily commitment. Now, you've got to balance that with the fact that much of your activity is about building long-term momentum and deeper networks, which might not make the cash register ring today. Still, most experts agree that checking in on your social networks once a day, and checking in on your blog network once a day (or every other day if you don't post that frequently) is necessary to maintaining a strong social media presence. Once you're up and running, you'll figure out which online friends and linked blogs are the most beneficial by checking your hits and updates.

So, what would a social media marketing focused program look like? Most major social network sites offer you the ability to do the following:

- Monitor discussion on social communities and networks for key conversations, keywords and topics
- Identify top concerns relevant to what your company is promoting
- Identify influential bloggers and authorities in the social communities, ask them their opinions
- Identify media types most often used with topics and communities: text, video, image, podcasts, blog posts, comments, microblogging, status updates, social network notes, social news and bookmarking and as possible, direct messaging and IM
- Create messaging specific to media type and platform as way of sharing information about your company
- Create content destinations that explain the offer and that also offer the opportunity to interact, share opinions and comments
- Reach out to influential bloggers on a one to one basis, recognizing them for sharing their opinion, explaining the offer and your goals. Ask them to help you spread the good word. Explain what's in it for them and what's in it for the community
- Polling: On several social marketing sites, you can seek out what people in your network might do or how they would respond to potential changes to your company offerings. This is a great way to conduct test scenarios without involving the general public
- Monitor the communications that result in the most signups and provide feedback on progress
- Offer influential bloggers a "free pass" to blog the event or a preview of what's being offered

- Recognize participation and contribution to reaching goals
- Continue to engage interested participants and communities

I know this might seem like a lot of work and possibly more effort than it's worth to a traditional direct marketer. But to those involved with social media and social communities, it's familiar territory. Your company can focus on developing solutions based on what the audience wants, then on involving the community in developing and promoting creates evangelists for the promotion. Recognizing participation energizes the community and can multiply the speed and breadth of message distribution, discussion and action.

Keep in mind that the appeal of social networking is limited largely to industries where workers are fairly isolated from their colleagues on a day-to-day basis, like medicine, construction and sales. Social networking might not be for you, but it's definitely worth looking into.

B2B NETWORKING DANGERS AND HOW TO AVOID THEM

Beware whom you refer and with whom you connect. The Internet is wide and can be anonymous. The John Smith you used to work with might not be the John Smith asking for a reference. Keep your name trustworthy by double-checking before you link yourself to everyone. Some sites might even be spam sites that want to build link farms- trust that your legitimate contacts will expand. Remember, trustworthiness is everything online. Anything that sets your standard above others, any respectable names you can connect to your own, make your business stand out.

Security issues become important to monitor once your company starts socially connecting online. In Web 2.0, as businesses are able to communicate with consumers in more varied and intimate ways, they have to find ways to be more engaging and communicate more directly to their customers and the public, while retaining close control of sensitive information. "Friends" that we once had at company X might now be the competition at company Y. When the relationships you have in your online communities get tangled you need to exercise caution in what you share or the consequences might hurt your company and/or your career.

Remember, "Google never forgets." Anything you do on the Internet is instantly passed along to everyone else in your network, and anything that gets posted and syndicated to other sites, or linked to any other site, can't be taken back. Sure, you can delete a blog post, or hide a negative comment, but anything you do on someone else's page is permanent! Before you post anything, double check not only the basic grammar and spelling, but how it reflects on your company. And if things go wrong, move the discussion to private e-mail, phone, or even face to face!

Also remember that business-to-business sites are more for inter-industry networking. If you run a construction company and you meet up with architects online, you can create partnerships to benefit you both. But these sites are not going to reach a broad audience of potential consumers. For this reason, spend less time on these sites unless you are a salesperson looking for vendors, or a service person seeking places to offer your services. Know what your goals are, then decide how much time to spend on each type of online marketing.

Social marketing invests in social communities with useful content/solutions as well as participation and recognition. That investment delivers long-term dividends far beyond a one-time promotional program using direct marketing tactics. Web 2.0 makes it possible for your company to reach interested parties in your field and in related industries in a variety of different ways. Invest just a little time to see which modes of connecting might be right for you.

And above all, remember that the Internet is very good at passing along info, but very bad at making sure that info is trustworthy. Stand out by being professional, and by connecting yourself only with those contacts you know are legit. A small mistake online can reverberate in a big way!

Chapter 8:
MySpace

I NEVER GOT MY OWN room growing up, never had a chance to put the posters I wanted on my walls, or put in that cool castle toy box, or play my favorite music at top volume. So when I finally had my own space, I made sure to decorate it exactly how I wanted (expect the personal swimming pool!). I wanted people who came over to my pace to know more about me by what I had in my room. And I knew that if I had a cool apartment, I would have more friends over. Now, the social media giant MySpace.com lets anyone build an online profile page that links them to other users. Decorate it however you want, and start inviting people to get to know you!

In any business, image is key. You have to control your image and put your best foot forward so that your guests can quickly learn about you, and get fascinated by your company. Social media sites like MySpace.com are a perfect place to do this. MySpace completely changed how companies can interact with consumers. If you have ever wanted to paint your walls in a way that says "Buy Here!", it's time to get a MySpace page.

A BRIEF MYSPACE HISTORY
Brad Greenspan started eUniverse in 1998, one of the earliest online communities that allowed people to play games, trade music, and find dates. MySpace grew out of that initial cluster of online community networks in 2003 to compete with, and eventually overtake, Friendster. Now owned by FOX, MySpace has over a million unique pages, allowing users to post blogs, music, events, video, and photos. MySpace also lets people find friends and create an online community.

MySpace became a wildly successful platform for groups and companies to post multimedia information. Bands, stand-up comics, visual and performance artists, theatres, art galleries, dance clubs, concert venues have all been able to connect to followers in a wide variety of ways.

You and your business can form a profile page, a group, or both, and start connecting to potential customers today!

CREATING YOUR PROFILE

You will want to create a company account by logging onto myspace.com and filling out all the appropriate information for your company. Choose to create either a profile or a group. There are pros and cons about creating both groups and individual profiles:

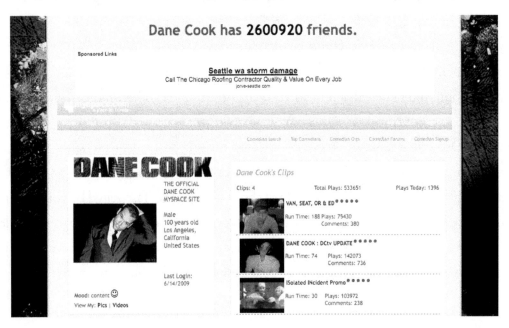

Figure 8.1: Comedian Dane Cook at Myspace.com

A PROFILE is designed for an individual and lacks the clear business designation. When you post as an individual, you will be asked for individual information like birthday and hometown, religion, etc. Deciding how to fill out these categories takes a clever hand. Best to be vague, or to just create a personal profile for yourself (being highly professional, of course), and then become a member of your company's group. However, being an individual does give you maximum control over what gets seen on the profile. Profiles clearly have one author, and allow you to control the whole look. The information on the pages cannot be manipulated by anyone but your MySpace administrator (at some point, you might want one).

There are, of course, some examples of people who have used their profile as a major source of their business, such as comedian Dane Cook (See Figure 8.1). Cook seized MySpace's viral opportunity early in the game, and keeps his young fans informed of his every move, which keeps them wanting more, and he delivers. So, if you are your brand, a personal profile is a great way to personalize your company.

A GROUP is different than your company profile (of course, if you'd like, you can post a personal profile as well to connect your friends who might search you out to your company site). If you log into your account you can create a group and modify how much access each group member has. Maybe you want to be the sole administrator, or you want to share the duties with someone. Just like with your blog, as you develop a wider social network, you'll need more time to keep up with it. Groups offer more access to a wider range of people, and you can look up groups on MySpace to see what is already out there in your field (See Figure 8.2).

Figure 8.2: Business & Entrepreneur Group at Myspace.com

Regardless of which format you choose, MySpace is a great place to build a Web presence. One of the two things that separates MySpace from a regular website is the clear layout, with some variation. MySpace pages all feature the same general information: who you are, where you are, what you do, a blog, a bulletin board, event calendar, space for photos, music, videos, and links to your friend's pages. But MySpace also offers applications to personalize the overall look of your page. The background, font, color scheme, music, and visible information can all be manipulated to match the brand of your company. You can place your company logo all over your page so that it is very clear that you are a business, not some college kid.

MySpace has been compared to opening a bedroom door—everyone has one, but when you open it you see the posters on the walls, hear the music they have playing, check out the pictures of their friends and family, and get a sense of the person by the general décor.

The other thing that separates MySpace from a self-designed website is its interconnectivity. Sure, you can include links on your site to create a network with other similar websites. But on MySpace, you are automatically hooked in to a network of hundreds of thousands of individual Web users. Rather than people having to seek you out, you can invite them to learn more about you, and with each new friend comes several new potential friends to whom you can reach out.

The elements of your profile

- **Name and Information**- You can include as much or as little as you like here. Put your company name, your phone number, address, and contact info, website, etc. Include all the different categories that someone might associate with your company; the Likes and About Me sections can serve as search keywords, allowing users to find you more easily.

- **Photos**- Your company logo should go here, or the photo of the front of your store. This should stand out, be recognizable even in a thumbnail size, and should match what is featured on your website.

- **Layout**- One of the great things about MySpace (and also the downfall) is that you can make the layout highly personalized, creating something similar to an individually designed website. To change the font, color scheme, background, and text options, browse around the Web for one of many MySpace profile editors. You can play around with what fits your company aesthetic (ideally you want it to look a lot like your website). Then, put in HTML code to personalize your site in the about me section of your info box. At www.RobertNoll.com, you can find out easy ways to personalize your profile, without having to search all over for html codes.

- **Media**- Music, video, and photos can all enhance the power of your profile. But keep in mind that the more media you have on your page, the longer it will take your page to load. If you do choose to put a song on your site, it will start playing as soon as the page fully loads, so be sure that your song matches your company image- and is in no way annoying! Videos of store products or customer testimonials are great, but again they do take a long time to load. As for photos, you can create several different photo albums, for Store Events, products, staff photos, etc. Striking a balance between too much media and not enough takes practice, but always err on the side of discretion. A little good quality media will make your page stand out, rather than cramming it so full of videos that it crashes people's computers. For bands, MySpace still rules for music, since it allows bands to post multiple songs so users can demo right from their profile page.

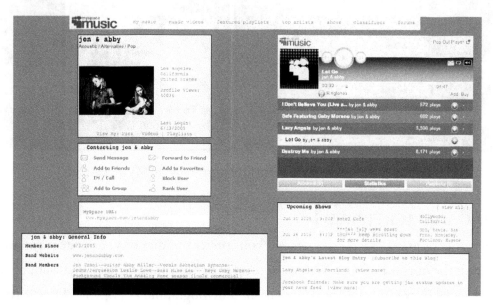

Figure 8.3: Musical group Jen & Abby at Myspace.com

- **Blog-** Ideally, you can get a blog software service that links your blog directly to this MySpace blog, so that you don't have to copy and paste constantly. Your friends can still subscribe to this blog just like they would do with your regular blog, so comment on relevant group blogs and start responding to comments that readers leave on your page.

- **Extras-** MySpace allows users to put calendars, links to other sites, and a wide range of promotional materials all on one easy to access page. Getting your own homepage to be similar to your MySpace profile will help users connect all the places you are on the web. For instance, if you let users buy tickets to an event on your company website, you can let them link to the same online purchasing tool from your MySpace page.

Figure 8.4: Rogue Artists theatre company at Myspace.com

MAKING MYSPACE FRIENDS

MySpace friends aren't exactly the same as your poker buddies or your college roommates. If you want the purpose of your MySpace group to be for your business, you want to extend your net wide, to cover as much of your desired demographic as possible. Don't just reach out to people you know, reach out to people who might be interested in you. Of course, reach out to people you know, but also consider who in your circle of friends might be able to put you into contact with a more focused group of potential customers. Just because your MySpace friends might not want to get a drink with you or go to your birthday party, doesn't mean they are not valuable in your social media network.

Who to contact

All those e-mail address you have from your lists of leads are going to come in handy again. Not all of these people will have MySpace accounts, but if your target demographic is under 40, odds are good that they have a MySpace profile. To find friends on MySpace (that's right, these people will be more than just leads- they'll be your company's friends!), you can search the MySpace network by name or e-mail. Send friend requests to the clients who have already agreed to be contacted by you. Then (and this is the real beauty of social media marketing), you can send friend requests to their friends, expanding your network exponentially.

Another great way to contact potential leads through MySpace is to check out the friend lists of similar groups and companies. Do a simple search for your company's main keywords and see who pops up. MySpace lets people list their interests, so check out people who have interest in your industry, and look through their friends to see if they are friends with any other related businesses.

You will probably also want to invite your employees to become friends, and any personal friends of yours, but beware: Depending on how professionally conservative your company is, you might want to screen your employee's friends or pages for appropriate content. Make sure your page is professional, since the very fact that you are on MySpace shows that you have a fun, hip, approachable, grass-roots side. Don't go overboard with the songs and non-business photos!

How to connect with your Friends

There are several features of the MySpace Universe, and you will want to use as many of them as possible to your advantage.

A. Friends- Just sending a friend request invites potential customers to check you out. Use the list of e-mails you have first to search for those people on MySpace. Then, once you have a profile, always ask people to become your friends on MySpace. Consider putting your MySpace URL with the rest of your contact info on business cards, brochures, listings, emails, etc. so people can get a more intimate look at your company online. Also become friends with other similar companies or local businesses by looking on their individual business websites and seeing if they have a MySpace widget so you can easily become friends with them in just one click.

B. Blog- You can host a blog on MySpace (and even link it automatically to your company blog!) that all of your friends can view. In fact, you can even notify friends when you have posted a new entry. Encourage people to subscribe to your blog, just as they would do with Atom or RSS outside of MySpace.

C. Bulletins- The sidebar with bulletin posts is a great way to publicize in-store events or special promotions. Make these short and sweet like your classified ads (Chapter 1). Bulletins often get crowded out or ignored, though, so always post several over time like teasers if they are for a single event.

D. Invitations- MySpace lets you create events and invite people, so you can easily organize a store event or a virtual event. If you want people to come to your holiday sale or if you want them to check out your online video chat session, send out an invitation easily to all your friends!

E. Commenting- Like blogging, keeping up on your social network is time consuming. As a company, you want to find a balance between keeping involved in your clients' lives, and overstepping your place in their private virtual lives. For instance, a great way to personalize your company is to send a Happy Birthday greeting, along with a discount offer. But don't comment on the fun birthday party photos they posted! As always, be professional.

MYSPACE DANGERS AND HOW TO AVOID THEM

It is important to remember that access to media all the time has its drawbacks, and Google never forgets! On the Web, *everything* is public, so make sure it's professional! Be sure that the layout of your page is cohesive with your brand image, and that the images and layout are easy to read and easy to load.

One negative consequence of the flexibility of MySpace layouts is that not all web browsers read them equally well. Ever tried to go to an individual's webpage only to find it completely un-navigable? MySpace allowed for two things to happen online:

1. EVERYONE had the same webpage format
2. Individual websites could connect to one another

But being able to manipulate the HTML code of the page allowed beginner programmers to change page layouts without knowing how different browsers were going to handle the code. Err on the side of simple: once your photo and logo, company name, and company contact info are prominent, be very picky about what else you chose to put on your profile.

Another small shift in your layout that can change your professional impact is making your top friends visible so you can network with other companies and group leaders. Shift your employees and related industry profiles to your top friends so that browsers can see to whom you are linked. You could even feature a top friend each month and make it an engaging contest. Just like with blogging always be on the lookout for ways to engage the customer rather than just transmitting information to them.

For a lot of businesses, creating a MySpace profile is an excellent way of keeping current and engaging the younger demographic. However, if your business offers a legitimate service or a product aimed at a broader demographic than 13-30 year old upper class trendsetters, you might want to stick with your standard website. MySpace is not for lawyers, banks, insurance agents, or to advertise real estate or medical supplies. Since MySpace is a bit chaotic, like an open-air market, if your business has credentials or requires gravity and authority, MySpace might not be right for you. No funeral home is going to have a MySpace profile!

But consider what your target demographic is before you rule out MySpace. There might be a new group you haven't tried to reach, especially as more people become tech savvy and more business is done on the Internet. Social networks like Friendster, MySpace, Facebook, Bebo, and others are the marketing platform of the future. So, if you want your hip legal service to get business from young pop stars or wannabe pop stars, consider a MySpace account. If you're a comedy promoter looking to showcase or represent the newest talent, definitely get a MySpace account. But unless you want "friends" posting their crazy spring break photos to your site, stick to more conventional online marketing platforms.

Chapter 9: Facebook

A FEW YEARS AGO MY brother and I were at our favorite weekend activity: we play basketball and he brags about his kids. One was just starting college and was getting very involved in a new social media platform called Facebook.com. He told me that all the cool kids were doing it, so of course I had to check it out as soon as we were off the court. Instantly, I recognized its cache came from being invitation only. Because membership was limited to college students, there was something hip, fresh, and cool about Facebook. But, like all things online, it was only a matter of time before access expanded and anyone, including a guy like me, could get a Facebook page and start making "friends."

Facebook is now MySpace's main competitor. Facebook.com is out in front of the social media race, which is where you want your company to be. Blogger Tameka Kee writes, "The latest Nielsen data showed some other striking shifts. In February 2008, Facebook didn't even break into Nielsen's top 10 list in terms of overall traffic; just a year later, its 65.7 million unique monthly visitors put it ahead of IAC (NSDQ: IACI), Wikipedia and even Disney (NYSE: DIS) (which it knocked out of the top 10 this year). It also beat both Google (NSDQ: GOOG) and Microsoft (NSDQ: MSFT) in terms of time spent." [2]

Yes, Facebook is now also used as a verb, as in "to Facebook someone," meaning "to look up someone's information via their Facebook profile, and make them your friend." Some people now even rely on their Facebook profile more than their regular e-mail.

How do you get your company to be part of the Facebook universe, so you can start instantly interacting with consumers online? It's easy, and highly effective, as Facebook has become the most popular social media site.

FACEBOOK: A BRIEF HISTORY

Started by Harvard students, Facebook has now become the largest social network on the Web. Unfortunately, part of what makes Facebook so great for the masses is also what makes it a little harder for marketers to use. But don't be discouraged! Facebook has just undergone some massive changes that make it easier for companies to create pages that are similar to individual profiles. Lost already? Let me explain.

Unlike MySpace, in Facebook's beginning, you could only join if you were a college student, and it you were invited by someone else. Eventually, Facebook decided to expand its usership, and now anyone can create a Facebook profile. But the basic design of Facebook is targeted to individual users, and the profiles are less customizable than MySpace pages are. Facebook profiles essentially all look alike in terms of layout, features, color scheme, font, etc., so it is a little more difficult to brand your profile with your company's image.

In the early Facebook days, just like creating a company MySpace page, you had to get creative if you wanted people to know you were a business, not an individual. But now Facebook has made it possible for a company to create a Facebook page, which is slightly different than a Facebook profile, but better for your company. Facebook pages offer you the option to open an account as a business, a product or service, or an entertainment entity/production company. The site lets you list your operating hours, link to a map, and detail your company mission statement. It's basically a webpage that has automatic links to other people, and that instantly alerts everyone in your network when it's updated. The main drawback of using your Facebook company page as your only website is that the format is standardized, so you can't create your brand as fully on its pages as you can on your own website. But it is a stellar way to connect your company to people, and to invite viewers to check you out, without making surfers find you, or having to e-mail hundreds of contacts.

SETTING UP YOUR FACEBOOK ACCOUNT

The first step is to go to Facebook.com, and get a personal account, though you can open a group page without a personal Facebook profile. Put up your profile photo, ideally your company logo, and a description of who you are and what you do. You'll pick which category your business is and fill out all the contact info. From there, you can add photos, video, link to other groups, and most importantly, FANS!

After you have a company page, consider your goals on Facebook. Do you want to use the company page as your own profile, or do you want to create a private, personal profile to separate your life and your work. It's a good idea to create a personal profile if you want more people to be able to find you, but it does compromise some of your professionalism. One way people will seek out your friendship is to use the search function of Facebook and see if your own name pops up. So, if people knew you in high school and are wondering what you are up to, they can type in your name, find your personal page, and from there be directed to your business page. HOORAY: a new friend!

With a Facebook profile, you add friends, but with a Facebook page, instead of friends, you'll start adding Fans. These people can check out your profile and read all the fun stuff you have going on. With the new Facebook setup, pages are more like profiles, and fans are more like friends. The main difference is that when your company page notifies its fans of something (store promotion, event, new product), they will all be notified at once, in detail. For companies with frequent events, such as the Upright Citizen's Brigade Theatre in Los Angeles, a Facebook page is a necessary way to let your web-savvy patrons keep up with you.

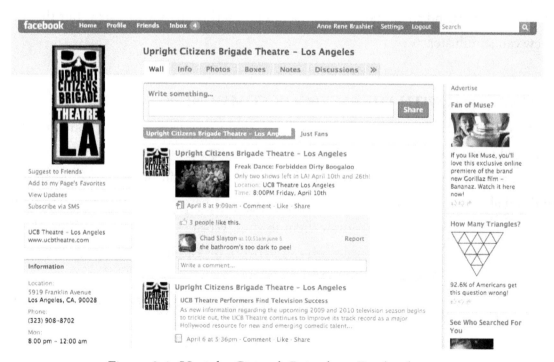

Figure 9.1: Upright Citizen's Brigade at Facebook.com

Groups

If your company is large enough to allow your employees to be a part of it, or if you are part of a trade group or small business organization, you should consider setting up a Facebook group together. This way you can all share information and events, and your clients can link together. When one company updates members, everyone in the group benefits with more page views.

Here's some information about forming a group: "Facebook founder Mark Zuckerberg noticed that the college students who make up most of his 9.5 million members were starting groups with names like Apple Students, where they swapped information about how to use their Macs. So he asked Apple if it wanted to form an official group. Now -- for a fee neither company will disclose -- Apple sponsors the group, giving away iPod Shuffles in weekly contests, making product announcements, and providing links to its student discount program."[3]

You can make your group public or private: if you have a huge staff, you might want to make a private staff group to keep employees in your loop. But the best way to involve other companies and all employees is to have a group that anyone can view, but that only a few can administer.

INTERACTING WITH THE FACEBOOK COMMUNITY

Congrats! Now you have a few friends and a place for new fans to learn about you. Now you need to work on adding more friends, building your social network. You relate to your friends and fans on Facebook much in the same way you will on MySpace. Keep them updated about what is going on in your company, and passing your information around, always looking for ways to either draw them to your website services or to you actual brick and mortar store. Here are the ways you can network on Facebook.

Finding Friends/Fans

First, you should have a few leads from your staff friends (make sure your staff adds you as a friend), and from your e-mail leads. You can also look in the following places for new potential friends:

a) Your friends' friends. Send friend requests to your most valued customers' friends. Odds are good, these people might know about you anyway from your friend-in-common. Capitalize on virtual word of mouth.

b) Related groups/ industry leaders. See who has become a friend of your national competitors, or become Facebook friends with people whose blogs you follow about your industry. Also search Facebook for interest groups in your niche, and send friend requests to their members.

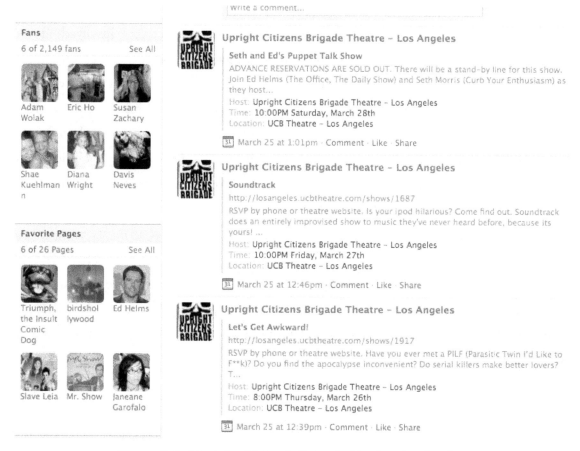

Figure 9.2: Upright Citizen's Brigade Facebook calender

If you want, you can search Facebook for people you know personally to become fans of your company. But make sure to check out if they will still be relevant contacts for your company. That grade school friend who now lives in Alaska won't have much impact on your small café in Ohio. But they might lead you to more directly valuable contacts. In the social media world, always err on the side to collecting more fans than rejecting them.

A note of caution; if you send out a large number of friend requests to people you don't know personally, you'll get a lot of denials from users who assume you are a spammer or setting them up with a virus. Make sure people can see clearly who you have as friends in common. Facebook automatically reveals your mutual friends, so try to have at least one mutual friend with someone before you send a friend request.

Updating your status

Frequently updating your status lets people know you are actively involved in the Facebook universe. If you can, I suggest logging into Facebook once a day and updating your status every other day. Keep your content fresh, and consumers will want to follow what you are doing. The Status bar at the top of your page should just be a short blurb about what is new, and should relate to other items on your website, Facebook page, blog, etc. "Company x is releasing new widgets this week!" or "Company x Holiday sale is now!" or "Company x likes this widget tutorial (YouTube url)" are all great quick ways for friends to see what you are doing right now. This is a bit like a Twitter feed, and if you have a Twitter feed, you can set your Facebook status to match your most recent Tweet (more on this in Chapter 11).

As a company, you'll want to update your Status very frequently. See Figure 9.3 for a company that does this well: the Los Angeles Contemporary Museum of Art. They are using social media to network with a hipper, younger, more connected group of potential museum patrons.

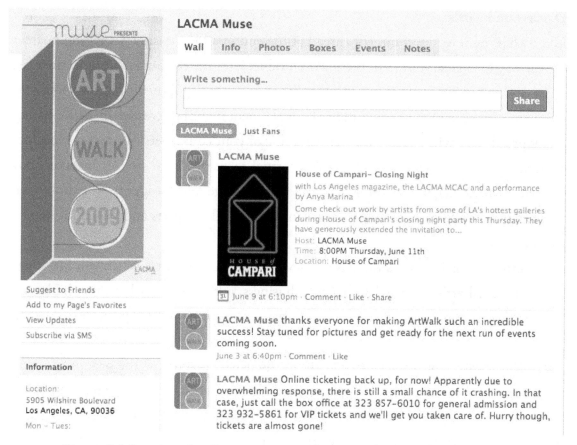

Figure 9.3 Los Angeles Contemporary Museum of Art at Facebook.com

Using Your Wall

This is a public message board where people can see what friends say about each other. Fans will write on your wall, and you can write on the walls of other people. One great use of the wall for your company is to write on the walls of other related groups and company pages, congratulating them on a big event for their company. The wall is like the comment scroll on your MySpace page. Be on the lookout here for negative comments or spam, and delete as soon as possible, dealing with the legitimate negative feedback in a private Facebook message to that person. Your wall will also show your recent actions, so only add friends and make comments that you want to reflect your company image. I suggest that you use your personal profile to tell your sister how cute her new baby is!

Discussion boards

Like a chat room or the comment thread at the end of a blog post, a discussion board is a great way to engage your customers. Post a topic, let some of your staff put in their two cents, and encourage participants in your Status. You can also let people know about your discussion in your blog or via e-mail. To make people more invested in participating, target people by inviting a specific demographic of your consumers for their feedback on a specific product or service. Use this as a virtual focus group to see, for instance, how your new widget helps single moms, or hikers, or college math students. The more exact you make the discussion, the more your fans will feel like experts and be willing to post to your topic.

Another discussion board topic is the news about your industry. When you find a new or controversial article that relates to your business, ask your fans what they think. And make sure you monitor this section well for spam. Also monitor it for great new ideas and potential contacts.

And of course you should participate in discussion boards for the groups of whom you are a fan. Leave the link to your site and let people link back to you if they find your comment insightful. Remember to be insightful, since there is an endless amount of information online, and you have to work to stand out!

Notifications

When your company is having a big event or promotion, you can send out a notification to your fans. This is a great way to give people a little more information about your news than the little status blurb. Notify your fans when you have published a new photo album, or added videos, or created an event. Keep them in the loop and let your fans know that you are busy. People are attracted to increased activity.

Facebook, like MySpace, makes it easy to invite fans to your in-store events and to your virtual events. Invite people for new product launches, special sales, discussion board topics, to the launch of new website features. One great thing about all online invitation sites is that you can see who has read your invitation and who has responded. Invitations are the most responded to feature on Facebook. So, if you do little else on Facebook, at least send out invitations to let your fans know about your latest news. In the informal virtual world, an actual invitation stands out as more legitimate and more urgent than other Facebook interactions.

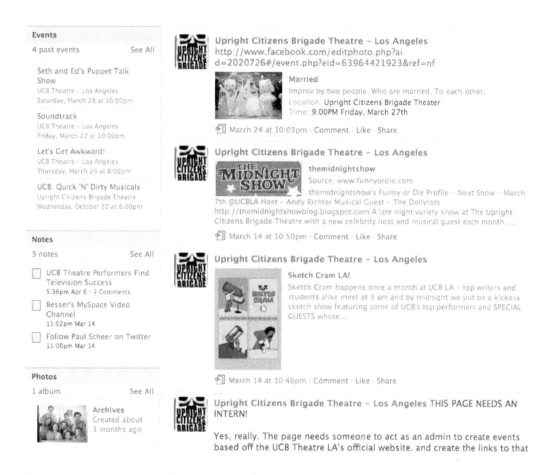

Leaving comments and tags on Facebook makes it easy for you to leave comments on other people's discussion boards, events, walls, and even photos. Plus, you can tag people in notes, photos, and videos, so when people in your network attend events with your company, you can easily share the photos with them. So keep a camera in your store and snap away, then get your customers' information so that you can tag them in the photos and befriend them.

Comment on anything you feel is relevant, and regularly look at the groups and pages of which you are a fan. There is a time balance to be struck here; unless Facebook is your business, be wary of how much you check out other group/ personal profiles. A simple comment with a link back to your site is sufficient.

Notes and messages

You can send a note to all your fans, which is a bit like e-mailing your blog post to everyone who might be interested. There is no good way to link your blog to your Facebook page, but you can post important blog posts to your Notes, and invite your friends and fans to read them.

Messages are really only used to privately communicate on Facebook. Since you want to use Facebook to create a very visible Web presence, messages are a great way to handle negative comments, or to help people with specific customer service issues. Quickly move these actions from the public sections of Facebook (your wall and discussion boards) into private messages. It shows that you care about the complaint, and it keeps your profile positive. Plus, if you help them out and they are satisfied, they can easily post a positive comment! You can even send messages to a large group, which makes it seem more personal than other forms of Facebook communication, more similar to an e-mail.

SPECIAL FACEBOOK EXTRAS

Because Facebook opens up its programming code to anyone, if you have a little tech knowledge, you can create an application that people can put on their own profile. These applications are the online equivalent to giving out free flashlights or key chains to customers. These can be games, or little virtual gifts users can pass on to their friends, and they can be a unique way to interact with your new social network. It takes a little time and computer programming skill, but can make your company stand out above the rest.

If you're not a computer person, seriously consider hiring a programmer to design a widget or application that people can use to promote your company. For instance, there is a travel website that created a game where people can design a map based on where they have traveled. Each time someone plays this game, the travel company gets one more chance to direct the user to their website, and make the user aware of their company. If you want to invest a little extra time and money (unless you happen to be a programmer), making a Facebook application is a fun, unique, eye-catching way to increase your Facebook presence.

Facebook is competing with MySpace's new marketplace, so now classifieds are social! There is a new section of Facebook allows people to post classified ads. Use this just as you would regular classifieds, but remember that this is mostly for individuals selling things, or for services. It's free, and it easy to use.

Another new development is FACEBOOK Connect, an application to put aspects of Facebook on your website. So if you want people to have more access to your Facebook applications while they are on your website, this can be a great substitute for getting a very expensive Web designer. It also offers immediate connectivity. If someone is on your company website and finds a service that interests them, they can leave a comment on your website that will show up on your wall!

Facebook is constantly under new development, just like Google. Remember to check out the companion website to this book at www.RobertNoll.com for all the latest ways you can market through Facebook.

FACEBOOK DANGERS AND HOW TO AVOID THEM

Social networking sites take time and energy. Your online friends might actually expect your attention, and if you don't have the time to be there for them, they'll find new friends elsewhere.

It can also be difficult to maintain professionalism, as with other social networking sites. The format of Facebook is more professional than MySpace, but be clear that your group/ company profile is not where you post your photos of your spring break vacation, and that your high school boyfriend doesn't post your old, dirty secrets!

Even if you spend an adequate amount of time building your network, don't be fooled into thinking that fans equal business. Having a huge number of Fans does not guarantee any return on investment. Since you can't really sell anything on Facebook (yet), the only tangible benefit from social media marketing is brand notoriety. The work is then up to you to decide how to use your Facebook friends. You could allow these contacts to sit there, more like acquaintances, or you can engage them in a way even more direct than your blog. With all the functions of Facebook, it's easy to find one that works for your business.

No matter how you choose to engage your friends, ensure that all your interactions remain professional. Overall, Facebook is more for personal use, not business. Remember, this is social media. You won't have the same amount of control over content that you have on your company website. Decide how to use this to your advantage, by engaging users on a whole new fun level without harming your reputation.

Some bands have allowed customers to design music videos, album covers, t-shirts, etc. The format on Facebook is so clear, that it's easy for people to interact with it and feel ownership of the brand. Again, this is very targeted marketing, so if you have a lifestyle service, Facebook is a great way to connect. If you have a more professional business, however, this might not be the best way for you; no psychiatrist gets credibility with a funny status update!

And, even on Facebook there is spam. Avoid being mistaken for a spammer by targeting just those who are connected to you in some way. Avoid getting spammed with diligence, checking who posts to your site. They will either be friend (someone to add) or foe (someone to swiftly delete).

Finally, the Internet blurs personal and professional, public and private, so be careful what you post and who else you allow to post to your profile. You don't need your accountant's inappropriate vacation photos on your site!

Increasingly, people are seeking information from search engines and seeking people and specific companies through social media sites. When you get on Facebook or MySpace, it's like being a part of a focused search engine where people can find you easily. And, once you find potential leads, you can target them with all your enticing information. From there, focus on moving people from Facebook to your company website.

According to ADAGE.com, "late last year Facebook started becoming a bigger source of traffic for some large websites, according to analytics firm Hitwise. It seems inevitable that, given Facebook's sheer scale (180 million registered users and counting), it would at some point start referring a lot of users to some sites, but the development is surprising. Web users go to Google to figure out where to go next; they go to Facebook to, well, hang out."[4]

SECTION 4:

NEW MEDIA

I MOVED NOT TOO LONG ago and took a lot of old electronics to the recycling center. Old phones, phone chargers, obsolete hand-held devices, dead laptops, and other archaic hardware that would make my nephews embarrassed. Technology keeps changing, and even if you're not in a tech industry, you have to keep up or get left in the trash heap. Now you can send a text message from your phone to another phone with a link to a video that someone can then watch while they walk around to get lunch. That means you've got to keep finding new ways to reach out and touch people. Now, remember, this book is not meant to overload you with information. Pick a few chapters, and experiment as your time allows. New Media is constantly changing, so check it out when you get some space in your schedule.

Online no longer means looking at text on a website. Now consumers can be online while they are watching television, playing video games, or on their cell phones. Our computers can stream video or broadcast television. Our BlackBerries can open up a map search while we are trying to find a restaurant. Now that you know the basics to free online advertising, it's time to get comfortable with some of the newer free sources of advertising at your fingertips.

Chapter 10:
Mobile Marketing

AH, THE OLD CELL PHONES that were just used to call people. Now I don't know what I'd do if I spent a day with out my cell phone. I lost it once at a busy restaurant and had to wait until the next evening to get it. That of course was the day I received 30 voice mails, as many text messages, and had to pull out an old paper map instead of relying on my map/ GPS application on my phone. My point is that your potential consumers rely on their phones. So be a part of that mobile network and you'll be a part of something they can't live without.

These days, a simple webpage might not be enough, as iPhones, BlackBerries, and other portable digital assistants become increasingly popular. People are on the go, and they still might want to check out your website while they go there. Be ahead of the curve by having a website specifically designed for mobile devices.

In this chapter we will describe how your company can go mobile! There are a wide variety of ways to reach customers while they are away from a computer. By establishing a marketing presence for people who are not constantly on their computers, you drastically expand how potential customers can interact with you.

Here are some basic ways to reach out and touch consumers on the go:

1. Your mobile website
2. Listings on other mobile sites
3. Text message updates

YOUR MOBILE WEBSITE

Phones are increasingly like little computers, with screens capable of showing text-heavy images. But keep in mind that your detailed website might not show up well on all mobile devices. If you've got a simple website that does not use video or online sales components, your site might not need an upgrade. But for those of you with more advanced websites, you might want to see if you can recode your site yourself.

To ensure that your site is easy for mobile viewing, add the mobile domain to your name: if your site lives at www.mysmallbiz.com, you're going to want to set up a sub-domain at mobile.mysmallbiz.com. How you accomplish this is usually pretty straightforward but differs depending on your host. Go to your domain host account homepage and, from their control panel, you can usually add subdomains easily. You want to set up your subdomain as a "mirror" of your main site, meaning the subdomain is really just pointing to your existing site. This works well if your homepage carries basic company info in a simple format. We can help you through this process at our website, www.RobertNoll.com.

However, if your main site is complicated and full of flash animation or multiple interactive features, you might want to create a fully separate mobile site. This is handy if you have music and video on your homepage, since most mobile devices can't handle that much information.

Having a good mobile website will be increasingly important as people move to smaller portable computing devices. Anyone who has ever checked a company website on his blackberry knows the annoyance a badly designed mobile site can cause, and the stress-reducing ease a well-designed mobile site can elicit.

LISTINGS ON OTHER MOBILE WEBSITES

Wherever your site is found online, it should be found on a comparable mobile website. People can now access Google, Yahoo! and MSN from their mobile phones, so make sure your site is listed on those search engines. Registering for these mobile versions of the main search engines is easy. Most mobile devices also have GPS map locators, so it's important for you to be listed on Mapquest and Google Maps for mobile phones. This way, consumers can easily find you when they are traveling. Allowing your listing to link to your website and to call you directly makes it easy for anyone to find you whenever they need to. You can get registered on the mobile versions of popular map sites by checking out the links on our website, www.RobertNoll.com.

Most of these devices can run Google Maps and their own map programs, so make it easy for people to find your listing on these map sites. Again, make sure you are registered on Google maps, and fill out as much information as possible about your business, such as phone number, hours of operation, website, and any reviews.

There are a growing number of online classified sites that will link your information to their mobile site. So, you can register your company website on a site such as inetgiant.com and they will add your site to their listings.

TEXT MESSAGE UPDATES

Text messaging is another great way to keep customers informed about your latest company news. A test message is usually a short text-only (no image) blurb delivered right to someone's phone. If you want to start using text messages to keep clients updated and engaged, you'll need to approach them like really simple e-mails.

First, you'll need a list of text message contacts. These can be potential leads or current customers. Since you're getting private cell phone numbers instead of business numbers or even e-mail addresses, people might be more hesitant to give you their personal numbers. But see below for ways to make sure that you are targeting your text messages only to those recipients who might want them.

Second, you'll want to go online and sign up for a program that lets you send mass text messages. These sites usually cost extra or can be part of your phone plan allowing unlimited text messaging. The rules for texts are changing rapidly, so check www.RobertNoll.com for the most current ways to test your customers.

Third, devise a system for what you want to send and what you want to say. There are a number of different purposes for which text messages are appropriate. It's up to you to figure out what mobile messages might be right for your company and for your clients. Below we'll give you some guidelines to follow.

Finally, much like e-mails and any other alerts, the more frequently you contact people, the more they will feel engaged and invested in your company's brand . . . up to a point, of course. Don't overload your customer list with excessive text messages. If they want to keep aware of your every move, they can follow you on Twitter (See Chapter 11).

Getting contact numbers

Not every phone number is going to allow texts, so don't simply try sending text messages to every customer phone number you have on file. The best way to ensure that you are targeting those consumers who want to be contacted by text is to ask them their preference and text contact info at any purchase point, or when you ask them to sign up for your mailing list. In most cases, the phone numbers will be the same as text contact numbers.

For texting, you'll need to create a list of phone numbers in the same way you procure e-mail addresses (See Chapter 4). Make sure you allow customers to opt-in. This is especially important when using text messages, as some phones do not receive text messages and others charge per message. If a customer wants your information in text form, have a separate space for that in your order forms, on your website where people join your mailing list, or at your store.

On your own website, it's a good idea to include widgets to get people to send reservations/ appointments / confirmations on their phones. That way, when people place an order with you, RSVP for an event, or make a reservation online, they have the option of getting a confirmation text message in addition to or in lieu of an e-mail confirmation. This is a great extra service to offer some of your clients, and it's free to you!

Sending mass text messages

There are a few sites now popping up that can help you manage your list of text contacts. Bloove.com and ClearSMS.com are two free websites that offer you the ability to transmit Short Messages (SMS, also known as 'texts') to a large list of supported phones. You can link directly to these sites from www.RobertNoll.com and build your message list today for free!

Help : Support & forum

bloove

Return to main page

| Features | FAQ | Supported Phones |

Features by platform	Nokia J2ME	SonyEricsson J2ME	Nokia, Samsung S60	SonyEricsson UIQ
Auto sync			+ *	
Contacts	+	+	+	+
Contacts on SIM	+			
Contact archive	+	+	+	+
Message folders			+	+
Message archive			+	+
Send message/Initiate call	+	+	+	+
Browser bookmarks			+	
Phone logs			+	
Speed dials			+	
Screenshots			+	+
SMS via POP3			+	+

* Please note that this feature is available for Nokia and Samsung S60 3rd Edition or newer mobile phones only.

Bloove plans	Free	Basic
Max. mobile phones per account	1	2
Auto sync enabled		
Max. archived contacts	15	3000

Figure 10.1: Text message site Bloove.com

Text messages in action

Since text messages are so brief and personal, it's best to just use them for alerts, notifications, and brief updates. Here are a few instances when sending a text works particularly well.

A. Sending confirmation texts lets clients know you care. Send a confirmation whenever someone has ordered from you or made a reservation for one of your services.

B. Send a thank you and maybe a discount offer for larger purchases. Also send thank you notes when someone new has added themselves to your mailing list, as soon as they express interest in your company.

C. Send announcements about upcoming promotions and sales, whether in your store or on your website.

D. Send updates when you have added a new blog post, new video, new product, or sent out a newsletter. Also let people know via text if you have been mentioned in the press.

In short, consider text messages another way to get an e-mail subject line out to people. Pique their interest and give them a specific action to take when they get your message. Should they come to your store, go online to see your new video, or pick up their newest order from you?

Staying consistent

The Internet offers instant communication. I know, we'll repeat it over and over in this book, but since your online clients expect immediate responses, you have to try to keep up! Communications such as Thank You's, Confirmations, responses to problems, etc., must be handled right away.

If you are sending out text messages for store events, promotions or seasonal discounts, send them out on a regular basis. If you don't have more than one text message a month, make up an event! This is a good way to know if you're engaging your client base frequently enough. Weekly texts are probably not necessary unless your business moves at a rapid pace or with quick turnover, such as stock investments or fashion photography. But in most business scenarios, send out text messages with company updates about as often as you would send out e-mails or put up blog posts. Keep in mind that these messages go to people's personal phones, so don't leave too many messages. On the other hand, don't be like that relative who only calls once a year. People might just forget your number!

Applications are the future of mobile advertising, but at this stage they might involve more money than you are willing to spend. If you have any knowledge of programming, you might want to create a fun game or application that will establish your brand in the minds of consumers. Similar to a Facebook application, these programs allow users to interact with your brand on a whole new, entertaining, useful, engaging level. Again, we're looking at engaging as opposed to merely transmitting.

The next step of mobile advertising for free is Twittering, also known as Tweeting. Somewhere between e-mailing and text messaging, Twitter might be all buzz or it might be around to stay. Either way, you do your company a disservice not to look into it. We'll discuss Twitter in detail in the next chapter. Hopefully now you've got a leg up toward connecting your brick and mortar store to your online presence to your customers' direct mobile phones. These days, you don't need a tour bus, company car, or expense account to go mobile with your company. You just need a little patience and a willingness to take some technology risks. Go for it!

Chapter 11:
Twitter

I KNOW, IT'S A SILLY name, but so was Google way back when. Now, it's only a matter of time before "Twitter" also becomes a recognized word in the dictionaries. First there was instant messaging, but then, as computers got smaller and phones got more versatile, Twitter was born. So, what is it? Twitter is an online program that sends SMS messages to mobile phones, connecting users to each other. A Twitter account allows you to very briefly update what is going on in your life (or in the life of your company). Twitter users write brief (140 or fewer) characters in response to the question "what are you doing?" These brief updates are called "Tweets," and if you want to intently follow what someone is doing, you can keep up with their Tweets on a minute-by-minute basis.

WHAT'S A TWITTER?

An online site, Twitter.com, creates a network so that users with accounts can send and receive messages online and on their mobile devices to a large number of readers. Twittering is similar to an RSS or Atom feed in that it spreads your information to others, and allows readers to follow your news posts. However, Tweets are more of a soundbyte, whereas a news feed offers the whole article. For this reason, Twittering is mostly personal at this time, though that's quickly changing. Don't let this new technology pass you by.

WHAT TWITTER CAN DO FOR YOU

Twitter is a simple concept: take the immediacy of Instant Messaging or Online Chatting, merge it with net-wide syndication programming, and make it mobile! So now, the short quick conversations you could have on discussion boards can be spread out for any interested party to read. The new blog posts can be summed up and updated for people who can't check their e-mail. Twitter can be an easy way to connect to your consumers that are on the go, traveling sales people, on-site managers who are away from their computers for most of the workday, or frequent travelers who are hard to pin down.

Here are some common Twitter marketing techniques:

1. Notify consumers of specials, in store events, and sales.

Tweets enable you to present a short blurb about, say, your Labor Day Sale, or a new shoe in stock, to anyone who follows your Tweets. Instantly! Disseminate information quickly to a large group of people. When there is an issue that everyone needs to know about, or a tip that you want to share, Tweet it. For instance, see Figure 11.1 for the Twitter buzz during Apple's latest iPhone launch.

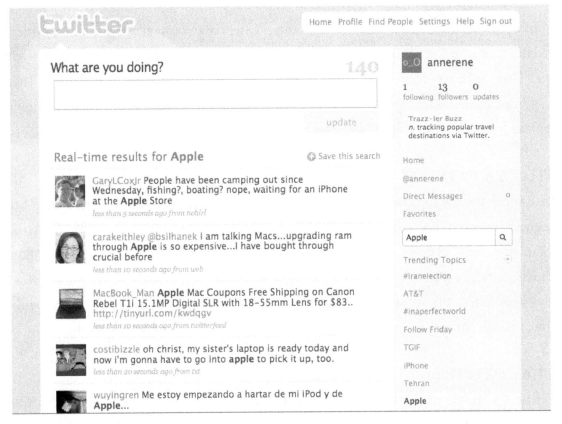

Figure 11.1: Apple buzz on Twitter.com

A great, instant alternative to e-mails, Twitter lets you grab your followers' attention by putting your store info where they don't expect it. Twitter is generally personal, so an invitation to participate in a promotion or to test a product has the feel of coming from a friend or acquaintance, as opposed to the generic quality of a mass email.

When a new product is being introduced, or when your website is down, or when you're adding tips to use new services, or even for sales and special promotions, Twitter lets you instantly contact your client base. One company that has used Twitter to its full potential is a Korean taco truck in Los Angeles. The truck offers late night food at several locations across the city. The hitch is, you can only find out when a truck is going to be at a location via Twitter. Creating an exclusive vibe is something that Twitter does well. If you want your followers to feel like they have VIP information about your company, Twitter is a great way to let them in on your little secrets.

2. Relate your business to larger news issues.

Is there a national company in your industry that just made news? Notify your followers. Did a governmental regulating industry just decide something about your industry standards? Let people know. Is there new research out, or did your product get mentioned in the news or in the media? Twitter can connect your company to the world at large, and remind readers of the relevancy of your company.

3. Give customers updates and feedback.

Is there a change in your store policy for service? New hours, childcare while you wait, a new specialist on staff are all great reasons to Tweet. If you have a great answer to a specific complaint, especially if it's a commonly asked question, a brief response can spread the word quickly.

Twitter can sometimes even reduce the amount of support calls. Many of these questions/issues are actually fairly straightforward, and can be resolved in one or two tweets. If these issues can be handled on the spot with just a little attention, you can really cut back on backlogging customer service reps.

Brief, simple customer complaints are perfect to handle on Twitter because they often allow others to learn and contribute along with whoever is asking the question. What's really cool about this is seeing other clients jump in and offer their opinions. If you get comfortable with your followers, and with the open sharing that WEB 2.0 services requires, you can establish your company at the forefront of consumer engagement.

4. Follow what people are saying about you.

Search tweets for your company, your product or service, and your competitors. Keep an eye on how often those tag words pop up on Twitter, and you can learn a lot about who is interested in what you have to offer. There are several sites that let you search for the most common keywords on Twitter, and to see if the people Tweeting about your specific industry might want to add you to their roster.

Generally, think of Twitter as an abbreviated blog or e-mail. It's a bullet point- you can flesh out the details in your actual blog or in a newsletter/ e-mail. Of course, each time you post something new on your blog, or send out a new e-mail or newsletter, or make a change to your company website, that's probably a good time to send out a tweet!

Best of all, since this technology is so new, it's up to you to discover new, creative ways to Twitter. Once you start exploring how some industry vanguards have harnessed the power of the Tweet, brainstorm what you can do! For instance, one small business tech software firm started organizing "Tweetups!" The organizer knew that most of the industry professionals working in the computer technology field would have Twitter accounts, so contacting them all by Twitter to arrange a networking night stood out among all the other invitations to events.

HOW TO TWEET WITH CONSUMERS

Twittering for your company is different than Twittering for yourself. For instance, if you have several personal friends who like to Twitter, you might want to get an account for yourself. Then get a separate Twitter account for your company that you and your staffers can update REGULARLY! This is the key to Tweeting successfully, just like blogging and social media marketing. Be consistent and people will want to follow what is new at your company.

Open a Twitter account and create a plan

Get Twitter accounts set up for yourself/staff and designate how often you all should Tweet. From our companion website, www.RobertNoll.com, you can go directly to the Twitter homepage and sign up for an account. A Twitter account is like the second half of an e-mail: @_____. For instance, your Twitter identity can be @LAfootdoctor or @brookespartyplanning. Make your Twitter name specific to your company, easily recognizable, and memorable.

Then, figure out who is going to be in charge of your Twitter account, and how often you will update it. Realistically, the brevity of Twitter means that you should update it at least once or twice a day; it only takes a few minutes.

You can update your account from any mobile device or computer, so whoever you allow to have access can upload to it anytime.

Build a contact list

Now you need to get people to follow you, which, of course starts with following other people. You'll need to add another step to taking customer and potential customer info to get twitter addresses. You can do this at your physical location in the same place people sign up for e-mails and give their phone numbers and addresses, and you can also do this on your website. Have an option to get Tweets where customer care appears on your website. When you ask for e-mail addresses at your store/ on your website/ blog/ mailing, also let people know that they can follow your tweets, and give them an easy widget to click to so they can do so.

Tweeting

On your phone you can Tweet anytime, anywhere, and it only takes a few moments. Because Twitter is mobile, your followers will expect you to Tweet frequently. The more engaged you are in the world of Twitter users, the more followers you will likely have. Since you are only inputting 140 characters, you might consider Tweeting once a day if your company rapidly changes. For instance, a financial consulting company might want to respond to current economic news daily, and at the close of each market. But if your industry moves at a slower pace you might only want to Tweet once or twice a week with general updates.

The key to Twittering, just like many other Web 2.0 platforms, is to communicate frequently and consistently. Fortunately, you don't have to be as inventive with your Tweets as you are with your blogs. A simple sales reminder or a link to a relevant article is enough to keep your followers engaged with you.

Tweets can be useful in collecting user comments about your business and industry. As you expand your online marketplace, you will develop a larger presence in online community. If you decide to put energy into Twitter, you will eventually want to use a service like Tweetdeck.com or another Twitter application which will sort Tweets by topic, so that you can find relevant Tweets on your industry in general, your company in particular, and news affecting your industry or town.

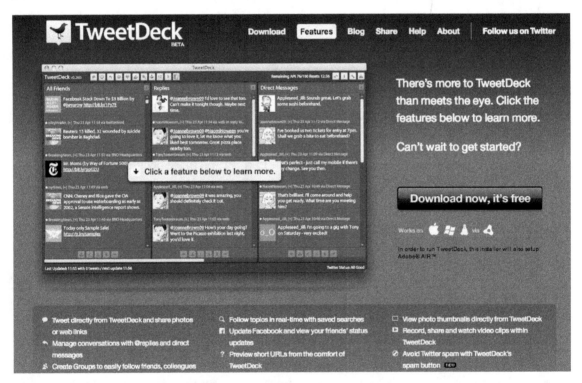

Figure 11.2: Organize with Tweetdeck.com

Seek out influential Tweeters in your industry and your city, and follow them. Obviously, start with the blogs you follow and your friends on social networks. You'll find some contacts who use Twitter more than Facebook, and vice versa, so make yourself available to all different avenues of communication.

TRACKING YOUR TWINFLUENCE

For successful Tweeting, find out how many followers you have and how may followers each of your own followers have; that is, how likely are they to pass along that they are interested in you to their followers? And are you actively engaged in listening to others or are you just shouting into the void? Twitter rewards those who listen and engage their customers- it is conversational in a formalized way. If you're just yelling into the void, no one will want to keep listening.

TWIT-FALLS TO AVOID

Like going into a crowded room an yelling "Anyone know a good way to make my vacuum work better?" Twitter allows brief, concise mass communication to a global community. But make sure that you aren't wasting loads of time in the void, chasing down followers on Twitter that won't become customers. Twitter has lots of pitfalls, especially because it's so new.

For instance, in order to reduce spammer access to Twitter, Twitter does impose limits on things such as how many people you can follow, how many tweets you can send per hour/ per day. You can't have too many more people that you follow in relation to how many people follow you. Once you start sending out Tweets to thousands of people, few of whom are interested in what you have to say, you're doing little more than spamming, and Twitter might even freeze your account. So make sure you have some dedicated followers; the best way to ensure that is to Tweet consistently, and to be informative and interesting when you do Tweet.

The thing about using Twitter (or other social media) for customer support is that by following dozens or hundreds of people, you can end up with a lot of updates regarding what so-and-so is eating for lunch, when you are there mostly for professional, rather than personal, purposes. Searching for industry/ company specific key words can really cut down on the amount of useless chatter you have to wade through.

Recently, Skittles had a great idea for using Twitter . . . that backfired horribly! They posted all the Tweets which mentioned Skittles on their website, hoping to reach consumers in a new, more immediate and irreverent way. Sounds great, until people started Tweeting inappropriate curse words and slander along with the word Skittles. The project quickly got scrapped after a few too many " I *@%#ing hate skittles in my &$$" were posted on their website. The moral of this story: be your own censor. The Internet is an immediate, rough, vulgar free speech zone, so tread carefully to maintain professionalism.

Regarding Twitter and customer relationship management, Twitter lets you listen to customers in real time. When there are support issues, you can deal with them more quickly than ever before. When there are feature requests, it's easy to gauge whether there is a groundswell of support for the idea. When there are complaints, deal with them immediately and, in many cases, put customers' minds at ease.

By interacting with customers on Twitter, you prove to them that you are really listening. Plus, it lets you respond to them quickly and personally. Twitter might not be worth your company's time and effort to follow others and stay plugged in, but it's worth checking out. If you want to firmly establish an ear to your movers and shakers, and to communicate directly with the trendsetters in your industry, it's time to start Tweeting.

Chapter 12:
Videos

WHEN A CO-WORKER SHOWED ME a ridiculous video of 2 men in lab coats putting Mentos candies into bottles of soda, I thought she was off her rocker. The elaborate videos were all over the internet, 2 scientists making grandiose displays of soda shooting out of bottles like geysers, set up in complicated displays and orchestrated to music. They were hilarious, but it all seemed silly until Mentos started paying them money to make these videos to attract interest in their company. That just goes to show you how one little video can turn into something much larger, thanks to the power of the internet to spread a popular item around.

Video advertising sounds daunting to many people, when in reality it's a simple, effective, and highly memorable way to market your company. This chapter will show you how to do it and offer some tips for success. There are many fun and easy ways to put your business on tape that don't involve actors or even a video camera! It is vital to your online marketing success that you get maximum exposure for your videos, via search engines.

Better than a network broadcast commercial, a web video can add dynamic energy to your Web presence. With every Mom and Pop shop setting up a website, video can really make your site stand out. Also, an attention-grabbing video can get passed around quickly, and if you make one that stands out, you can really jumpstart your Internet presence.

Now, we'll not only give you some clear examples of how online video can help you market your company, we'll also outline how to make a video on a shoestring budget, and how to avoid some of the worst online video dangers.

WHAT VIDEO CAN DO FOR YOU

There are many ways you can use video as an online tool to market your products and services. One is to showcase product usage. You can create a video to explain new uses for your product, or clarify how to use your product. Showcase the product in action, and give lessons on all the different ways customers can interact with the product. Educational videos follow an easy template, and a good lecture demonstration video can establish you as the expert on your company.

Testimonials are also a wonderful use for Internet video. Get some video cameras and some valued customers, some basic copy, and let the real people who value your brand speak for you. Internet video can bring the personal and genuine to the small screen. Testimonial videos are a great low-budget way to make a strong video for your company.

Consider creating video reviews of your services and products by industry experts. Seek out the people related to your industry who have review blogs or popular websites. You can get some real traction depending on who uses your product and gives it a great video review! Sugar Hair Salon puts some fun videos from their store events in an easy to locate place on their website (See Figure 12.1). You can check out several other good video website examples at our companion website, www.RobertNoll.com.

Another great thing about free online video is that it allows you to broadcast media advertising without network buying! The same ad that you might pay thousands for on television can be broadcast for free online. Plus, when you broadcast something on television, you have to choose where and how often to air it. Air it on the wrong station, or in a bad time slot, and no one sees it. When you post a video online, people can find it at any time. You can run the same ad you created for television for free anytime, plus people can link to it and forward the video to others.

Hopefully you've gotten some ideas for what you want to say in your video, or a few ideas to start with. Now, let's discuss how to produce it. From writing to uploading, here are the nuts and bolts!

Figure 12.1: Video from sugarhairsalon.com

HOW TO MAKE YOUR VIDEO

If you've got the ad budget to run a commercial, you can use the same spot you already created for television. But, say you don't have the capital for that quite yet. Thanks to some very user-friendly software, you can now create a video yourself and upload it to the Internet for free. First, start by figuring out what type of video best suits your company. Product usage videos, reviews, testimonials, and funny shorts can all be useful. If this is your first time putting a video spot together, start simple! There is a wide range of ways to make a video, but there are a few basic steps to know that will make the process easier.

1. Writing the content

Make it short, informative, funny if you can, and professional above all else. Three minutes or less, preferably less, is best. YouTube.com lets you post up to 9 minutes, but if you can't get the viewer's attention in the first minute, you may as well give up.

Think about who your main audience will be. If they are an older audience, stick with a more standard testimonial. They should be able to find your video easily, follow the information to your company website, and should know a little about you when they find you. More web-savvy audiences are very used to a variety of types of advertising spots, so be creative, funny, even outlandish so long as you clearly lead viewers to your website, your product, or your store.

If you feel unsure about what to say, it's easy to compile the basic information you would put on your website or in an expanded classified as into some jazzy copy. Or, since you've already been establishing your Web brand with a blog, e-mail newsletters, and social media, you should have a sense of what you would like people to see when they first interact with your company. If you keep it simple, even a 30 second video can have a big impact.

You should be clear about what action you want viewers to take after they have seen your spot. Can they go right to your website for more info? Is there a physical location with a special in-store event? Did you just get a service reviewed in another media outlet that they can check out? Or do you just want them to get excited about your brand? Be specific so that your viewers will know what to do now that they've heard of you.

2. Shooting and producing your short

Get a decent camera, get a good sound person, and keep it simple! You don't need a lot of special effects to grab attention, but a clear, concise message is crucial. Don't be afraid to make a bold statement, since you only have a few seconds to grab the viewer's interest.

If you are doing multiple product information spots, consider shooting them all the same day. Say you own a kitchenware supply store, and you have set up the lights and sound for a kitchen shoot where you explain how to use several different cooking tools. You can easily shoot 5 or 6 little shorts and suddenly fill your website with multiple videos.

It's wise, if you feel comfortable on camera, to get your face out there. You can establish yourself as the expert in your company this way. However, if you are not an aspiring actor, consider asking one of your more articulate sales representatives to be the star of your video. Or, if you want to give viewers an inside look at the family of your staff, see if multiple members of your team are interested in being a part of your shoot.

If you are really on a shoestring budget, check in with local community colleges to find crew people, like a cameraperson and lighting and sound experts, who would love to work for free so they can build their reels. Otherwise, ask some of your staff or friends to run your camera; a few extra hands on shoot day can really make a big difference.

3. Editing and configuring your video for the Web

Edit your video yourself with built in software on your computer if you have it (iMovie is the basic Mac program). If you plan on making multiple videos for the Internet, you might want to invest in a basic video editing program like Final Cut or Avid. Or if you really want to get it off your hands, you can find an editor either within your company staff, or by hiring an outsider. Again, this is a great job for a community college student who is in need of practice and who might work for free. Keep in mind that editing frequently takes a lot of time, so assume an extra month after you have shot your video just to be safe.

As you work with your editor, you need to start thinking about where you want to put your video. There is a wide range of options, and you will want your video to be broadcast in the highest quality wherever it is. As you finish editing the final cut of your video, work with your editor on compressing and exporting it to a wide range of sites. But for each place you post your video, remember that it takes at least an hour or two to format your video for each site. So pick your locations wisely, just as you would in choosing your physical store locations.

Our website will give you links to step-by-step tutorials so you can edit your video. It's a complicated process, and will depend on which video format you use to record, how many shots you have and how you shoot, and what software you have. If you record a simple, single shot, single take video blog entry onto a webcam directly into your computer, you can easily upload your video onto your computer and then directly onto a video player. You will still need to compress it for streaming, for which you might need a video compression tool such as Total Video Converter or MPEG Streamclip. You can download these programs for free and our website has links to help you use them.

VLOGGING

Vlogging is the most basic type of video production you can do for your site. Simply buy a webcam or learn how to use your computer's webcam, and start talking. Keep in mind that since this is the most basic video mode, it can also be the least interesting and least professional. But if you have a great charismatic personality, you have a lot to say about your company, your blog has several readers, or you have a wide and active social network, you might want to become a vlogger.

It will just be you and the camera, so talk right to the lens, be animated, speak clearly, and really engage your audience. This is not your average lecture, but you can take a note from Ted Talks, where the focus is on information, not spectacle. Short (a minute or less) vlog entries can be interspersed with slides to create a virtual power point presentation.

If you really have a small video budget, but have some time to play on your own and like to write and speak about your company, you might be a great vlogger. You can reach viewers on a very personal level this way, and save lots of money on crew, equipment, and other production costs.

WHERE TO POST YOUR VIDEO

There are tons of places online where you can put your video. The most obvious one is your own website. Think about where to put videos on your page. If you can host video right on your site, I highly recommend having a basic grabber video on your homepage, such as the player Vimeo.com offers. When people get directed to your site from search engines or links, having a video upfront will make your site stand out. If you have several videos, or as you make more of them, you might want to spread them out. Keep the one on your homepage as a basic grabber/ informative video. Then, consider including video tutorials on the product pages or creating a testimonial video page.

The downside of streaming video on your own website is that you need expanded bandwidth to support viewing. You want your media player to stream video quickly so that viewers don't have to wait forever for your video to load. Increasing your bandwidth costs, so here you have to weigh your opportunity costs. If you only have one or two brief videos for your site, you can get away with a simple media player. But if you are planning to put multiple videos on several pages of your site, you might want to get advice from your webmaster. The right compression rate and enough bandwidth will ensure that the film plays right when people click on it.

When you put it on your site, make sure that they have to click to play, so that the video does not start playing right away at full volume. No one wants to be bombarded without electing to view. Remember, the Internet is all about consumer choice, so work with consumers and allow them to choose to say "Yes!" to you.

YouTube.com and other popular sites

YouTube.com is one of the most popular video hosting websites, so when you make your video, you will certainly want to post it there. You will need to set up an account on YouTube.com, which is easy to do at their homepage. If you plan on posting many videos, consider creating your own YouTube channel. One nice feature about YouTube is that you can post your video to a few private viewers, preview it to check the final cut, then broadcast it at large.

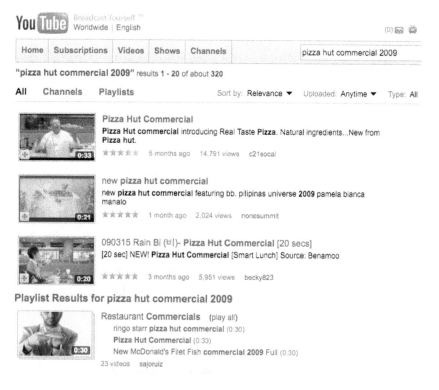

Figure 12.2: Youtube.com

Social Networks such as Facebook and MySpace also allow you to post video on your own profiles, and on the profiles of your friends. When you post a basic video about your company, put it on the homepage of your MySpace profile and in your Facebook videos section. Remember that these sites all have different specifications for how to upload your video, so make sure that you have the ability to convert your spot to a variety of compression rates.

When you visit other blogs, you can embed your new video within your comment on that blog. This takes a bit more html knowledge, but it's easy to learn if you have some time. Adding a video comment to someone's post can make your note stand out, which can drive traffic to your own website. Add a video when you comment on your social networks as well. That way, your friends will all be updated when you post a new video, and they can watch it instantly. Make it easy for people to view your video by making it short, knowing how to embed it so it loads quickly, and posting it to a wide audience.

GOING VIRAL

The World Wide Web is *so* wide that you have to broadcast your video on as many different media outlets as possible. These include blogs, newsletters, your website, social networks, alerts on Twitter, YouTube.com, and any relevant press releases. Reach millions of viewers for free by simply letting them know about your video and making it easy and exciting for them to watch it. The key to getting lots of viewers is to promote your video. Unlike a broadcast commercial, people rarely happen to catch an online video spot. You have to direct their attention to your brilliant commercial; otherwise it will go unnoticed.

Each time you create a new video, send out a newsletter e-mail to your loyal customers. Provide links to where the video is posted so they can view it easily, and let them know a few words about it. And when I say a few, I mean, a brief sentence about what the video says: is it funny, informative, about a specific product or promotion?

Make the videos easy for people to embed on their own blogs, social sites, and websites. Also, make them easy to share via e-mail, so that people can link their Twitter sites and e-mail them to friends.

Anything a step above average in terms of production value goes above and beyond what people expect from the Web, so this will stand out. Also, remember that humor always pulls people in and can help you humanize your company. Be creative, but remember that for most videos, standing out in the crowd is a tricky balance between trying too hard and not trying enough.

Flickr.com is a great site for multimedia marketing! Share videos and photos with interested parties. Your newest wine tasting, your recent location opening, your product line, etc. All these should be clearly searchable and easy to sort, and eye catching.

It's also important to make sure your video can be easily discovered through YouTube search. Your videos should have clear titles, an accurate description and appropriate keyword tags so that they can appear correctly in a YouTube search. YouTube Insight helps you figure out which blogs are directing traffic to your video and where your viewers live. For instance, if your video is popular in Brazil you can add a tag for Brazil so it will pop up in searches there.

Attaching your video to other popular video content is another way to make real video waves. For instance, the webseries, LonelyGirl15, got its legs by posting itself on the comments section of a popular, related blog. Also consider parodying popular videos, because when people search for that popular item, they might stumble upon your content. If a video is popular, YouTubers often race to create 'video responses' that will then appear next to the popular video. A great example of that is a video highlighting a glitch in an Electronic Arts' video game that appeared to show a pixilated Tiger Woods walking on water. In response, the game-maker posted a video that showed the real Tiger Woods literally walking on water, which attracted a far bigger audience than the original video.

If you can create good content and give people a sense of insider discovery with your cool video, you have struck the online video sweet spot. A sense of discovery can be built by attaching your video to other online content. But this is a bit more risky, as you are relying on others to love your video and pass it on. The best bet is to cast your video promotion net wide.

TRACKING YOUR PROGRESS AND FEEDBACK

Now it's time to determine if your video production is improving your returns. If you don't have a big budget for web analytics, you can see who has viewed your video when you log in to your YouTube.com account. This will show you how many views your video has on YouTube. You can't see who else has viewed your video, but it's a start.

On social media sites like Facebook and MySpace, you can let people "Like" your video. They don't have to comment, they can simply give it a positive rating. This is an easy way to see if your video is getting viewers.

Ask for comments within your video, and request feedback from them. This will also give you a good idea of how many views your video has. On your own site with a little analytics knowledge, you can see how frequently your video has been streamed.

Videos get feedback if they ask for it. If your video makes a real impact on viewers, they might even link to it on their own sites, or pass it on. However, not all of the comments you get might be glowing reviews. Respond right away, and if the complaint is particularly egregious give them a clear customer service path so they can contact you personally. But it's a good idea to respond even to positive comments with a simple "thank you!" so that the online world knows you are listening. Again, don't just transmit your information; engage your audience in an interactive way.

DANGERS OF ONLINE VIDEO PRODUCTION AND HOW TO AVOID THEM

Always avoid making your video overly long. If you can get your message across in a minute or less, do it! If you did it in 5 minutes, but you can do it in 3, edit your film down to 3 minutes. Include a counter under the video so that people know how long it is, and what they are in for. Net Surfing attention spans are shorter than even television viewing attention spans.

Think about keeping your design consistent. If you don't consider your visual scheme, you won't have one. Your video needs to project a consistent image of your company. If this image is not thoroughly consistent, down to the smallest details of all of your public communications, your company will appear to be amateurish, unreliable, improvised. The exception to this rule is if you have a specific concept that focuses on your company brand as hip, loose, improvised, and offbeat. A skateboard shop will want a very different style video than a law firm. But even in this instance, the video style is consistent with the skate company's brand image.

Beware of other people using your name or product in their videos! Monitor your company name as it appears in searches for videos. Make sure you know the laws about your copyright protections and libel/ parody protections if other people use your work. Conversely, make sure that you are not using content illegally. Be careful what music you use, and check with copyright laws in case you want to include a clip from a related movie or television show. The best way to avoid copyright infringement is to make your spot 100% on our own.

There are many types of videos you can choose to create for your company:

Testimonial

Product review

Video blog

Re-broadcast a traditional commercial

Educational video

The most important thing is that you have at least one video, preferably on your homepage, and elsewhere on your site and online if possible. Make it short, snappy, informative, and eye-catching to start establishing a real media presence.

SECTION 5:

WHAT NEXT?

IF YOU ASKED ME TO name the most significant technological advancement in my lifetime, I could say the Internet, or personal computers, or television, or space travel or wireless technology, but really the list is endless. You can't fight change; you have to embrace it! I know some information in this book will be obsolete as soon as you buy it, but that's why you can always check back in on www.RobertNoll.com for the latest small business online marketing news.

Technology constantly evolves, and it can be hard to keep up, especially if your main business focus is not related directly to the Internet. But we're here to help. If you have found success with our suggestions, GREAT! Now it's time to take your game to the next level and consider investing in a Pay-Per-Click advertising plan.

You might be happy with the free advertising strategy we've helped you build. But you might also want to stay on top of the latest online marketing trends. We've compiled a useful list of resources for you on www.RobertNoll.com, in addition to other helpful hints you can find there.

Chapter 13:
Pay Per Click

It all started with a lunch, a bottle of good Cab, and a conversation. A friend met me at a local restaurant for lunch one afternoon several years ago, to catch up and also discuss business. He expressed to me his concern about the amount of money he was spending on advertising. At that time, he was spending twenty to twenty five thousand dollars a month on radio, and the results were horrible. What was once a powerful advertising medium for kids and teens was now relegated to the ashes of history, losing much of the impact they once yielded. He knew I was knowledgeable about the Internet, and asked if there was any way this knowledge could help his business. As lunch progressed, the conversation shifted its focus to pay-per-click advertising. At that time, I had a very vague understanding of it, but was anxious, nonetheless, to better acquaint myself with this platform and see if it could help my friend. We both left the restaurant with guarded optimism that perhaps we had discovered something incredible.

Armed with a limited amount of knowledge, I spent the weekend studying Google's Pay-Per-Click section called "AdWords." By Monday, I had designed a landing page and built an Adwords Campaign for my friend's business. I called him on Wednesday morning and said, "I think I'm ready to go live! Let's see what happens." Shortly after, the flood began. The leads that my friend needed started to flow-in at an amazing rate. More importantly, the vast majority of the leads were looking for the exact services my friend's business provided! Realizing I was on to something, I decided to test the program out further, expanding to other industries that thrive on leads. That was the start of Monster Pay-Per-Click, a small (by choice) boutique Internet marketing company specializing in lead generation.

Understanding the core basics of pay-per-click advertising is important for any business owner, be it that of a small, medium or large establishment, considering delving into the online advertising world. The goal here is to help you determine whether you should do it yourself or hire a professional company to handle it for you. There are many problems and pitfalls to overcome if you decide to go it alone, so start with a basic understanding of this incredible advertising miracle that will rule for years to come.

IMPORTANT TERMS

Let's start with the basic, fundamental terms you must know and understand:

1. Impressions: An advertisement's appearance on an accessed Web page. Advertisers use impressions to measure the number of views their ads receive

2. CPM: Stands for "cost-per-thousand." Ads that are priced on a CPM basis are charged a certain amount for every 1,000 impressions their ad receives.

3. CTR: "Click-through-Rate" is simply the number of clicks divided by the number of impressions. A 3% CTR or above is considered very successful. Under 1% and it's back to the drawing board.

4. CPC: "Cost-Per-Click" is the amount of money you will pay for a single click on a pay-per-click advertising campaign.

5. Conversion Rate: The percentage of visitors that convert to a sale or a lead from a pay-per-click campaign.

6. Keywords: Exact, Phrase, Broad: Think like your customers. What search term or terms would they use to find your business or service?

7. Links: A link from another related website to your website—usually this is reciprocal. Google views them as a positive vote for your site.

8. ROI: Return on Investment. How much new business you generate for each dollar spent on advertising.

9. Content Advertising: Google, Yahoo and MSN display ads on Web pages of site owners participating in and signing up for split commission services. For example, NYTimes.com, About.com, Business.com, etc. all advertise on partner sites who

share revenues. These are very different than search engines and can be much more expensive if you don't know much about them.

10. Search Partners: On Google they include Google Product Search, Google Groups and websites like AOL, Netscape, CompuServe, etc.

11. Conversion Tracking: Code placed on a "thank you"/confirmation page allowing you to track and monitor the number of leads or sales are gained from the number of impressions.

12. CPA: "Cost-per-acquisition." To me, this is really all that matters. What does a sale cost? This statistic determines your budget and anticipated profits. If the sale is $1,000, you have a lead cost of $5.00 and are converting 5% of the leads into a sale, your acquisition cost is $100 per-sale. Not bad for a service industry.

13. Google Slap: One morning you will wake up and your campaign's minimum CPC will have gone from $0.60 to $5.00 or even $10.00 a click. This is Google's penalty for advertisers who have landing pages and site with insufficient content.

14. Quality Score: Far from an exact science, but overall, the search engines score your landing page and advertising copy used in your pay-per-click campaign.

GOING IT ALONE OR HIRING HELP

Even if you hire an outside company to manage your pay-per-click campaigns, you should at least completely understand all of the following. The decision to build the pay-per-click campaign yourself or let a professional group handle it for you is a big decision, and one that should take some deliberation. Pay-per-click can be expensive depending on your budget, market, competition, and many other factors. In my opinion, if your budget is in excess of $2,000 per-month, hire a great Internet marketing firm. The exception is if this is going to be your full-time job. Regardless, there is always something a pro can contribute aside from his expertise and his ability to see things that you will not. Pay-Per-Click can be incredibly time and labor intensive, so keep that in mind when considering hiring a company. Remember the story about the king sending his men out to collect all the knowledge in the world? They brought back tens of thousands of books, and then narrowed it down to a thousand, then to a hundred, and this was still daunting. One soldier suggested narrowing it down to one section. There is no free lunch! You are either going to pay in time or in money, but you will pay. It is up to you to decide what will be the cheaper, more effective way to build your business.

If you decide to go further and handle your own campaign, here is what matters most:

1. Relevance

I can't stress enough what this means for a campaign. This word is the single most important factor in any Pay-Per-Click campaign and deserves to be treated as your top priority. By making your search relevant, you lower your cost-per-click and insure a much higher conversion rate. Put yourself in the searcher's shoes and in Google's shoes as well. If you were searching for a "foot doctor in Los Angeles," you want exactly what you are looking for, nothing more and nothing less. You don't want a foot doctor with an office in San Diego. Google wants you to find exactly what you are looking for and have a positive search experience. To be relevant, always remember: content is king! The more strategically placed your content is, the better for you, Google and the searcher.

2. Keywords

Advertising copy is an art and very few excel at this aspect of marketing. On Google, you have only 25 characters for your header, then two lines of copy, each limited to 35 characters and finally, 35 characters for your URL. With these limitations, you had better be an artist because you have very little space to paint a picture in order to evoke a response from the searchers. I'll make this brief but concise: Start with the header. Make certain the search term is in the header wherever possible. If you don't, you will pay for it in higher click-through costs for a lower position. The body of your copy should start with your high points and end with a call-to-action. Last, your URL should make a statement about the search experience as well. Don't follow the rules and you will proceed at your own peril. Google is strict and they take no prisoners. Understand this from the very beginning and you can prosper.

There are many keyword tools available for free that can greatly assist you in reaching your goals. However, I think you are better off just using Google's free tool in the beginning.

Although not perfect, it is user-friendly and very helpful. Think about it, if anyone knows what Google wants, it is Google.

3. Your landing page

Landing pages are another art form and will play a major role in determining your success. Obviously, you want a page, preferably part of your website that engages the searcher. It should answer the searcher's questions and give them an opportunity to interact by filling out a form or purchasing your product. Color, animation and verbiage are all critical aspects of the page and should be chosen carefully. If you are looking for leads, keep in mind that the fewer fields a user has to fill out, the more conversions your site will get, period. Here again, Google is very strict about their criteria. Besides having bots visit your site, a human will eventually show up to rate you and refine your quality score. This is where the final decision for the searcher is made. To fill out or not fill out; to buy or not to buy; to stay or to leave-- ultimately, their choice is a direct result of your effort.

Testing, testing and more testing is a large part of any pay-per-click campaign. Google doesn't trust you yet if you're new. When you consistently test various advertising copy, keywords and landing pages, Google will see you are in it for the long term. Testing can save you a fortune in the long run, so be willing to spend the time, effort and money to perfect your campaign.

4. Bidding

Last, bidding is another art form. With a keyword like "DUI Attorney" costing over $20 for a decent position on Google, you better know what you're doing. Clicks today cost a fortune and usually, over 30 companies are bidding for the same position, and sometimes hundreds. If you can't afford the first page, let it go. You won't get appreciable results.

The bottom line is, pay-per-click campaigns take a tremendous amount of skill, knowledge and time. It became my specialty, according to one of my brothers, because I grew up reading daily racing forms! The objective is almost the same—win, place or show, and get the largest return on your investment. For those of you who aren't going to study pay-per-click, hire an outside professional and save yourself a lot of time and money.

Chapter 14: What Next?

Now that you've got your feet wet in a few areas of online marketing, we encourage you to keep up with all the new relevant technology on the web. We can help you navigate the evolving Internet marketing chaos at www.RobertNoll.com. We've even got a checklist for business owners who want to keep their online advertising campaigns growing in an organized, clear way.

Every resource needed to initiate or expand your advertising campaign is one click away! Whether you need an email service provider or a specialist in pay-per-click, by visiting www.RoberNoll.com, you are only one click away from links that fill all your free internet advertising needs.

My last words about all of this are extremely important: You can live by the Internet and you can die by the Internet! Not each platform is right for everyone, which is why we suggest picking just a few chapters at first and testing out the ROI for different methods.

If you start a social media campaign, say on Twitter, you can't just stop – the damage to your brand can be considerable. Once started, you must devote time, energy and research to your postings. A good idea is to set aside a particular time of the day to address the matter, sit down and do it. Keep in mind that there are some controversial businesses that should avoid any and all social media advertising. They tend to get quickly killed if the spotlight is on them. Ask yourself: *Could this advertising venue harm me in any way? Could this, over time, turn into a negative experience for me or my business?* The bottom line is this: choose your media thoughtfully. Look at the possible unintended consequences of your marketing choices.

We hope we've been able to help. Please let us know how we've helped you grow your business. For continually updated information about Internet advertising, you can always check back to www.RobertNoll.com for the latest online marketing research. May your online future be bright!

GLOSSARY

API: Application Programming Interface, the code that allows you to insert an application from another site onto your desired page

Bandwidth: the amount of data a network connection can carry in a given time duration

Blog: an abbreviation for "web log", an online journal similar to a running op-ed column

Blogger: an author of a blog, esp. one whose chief profession is writing the blog

Blogging: to update and maintain an online journal

Click-through: when a user clicks on a link or prompt on one webpage, causing another page to open

Conversion Rate: the percentage of visitors that convert to a sale or a lead from a pay-per-click campaign

Conversion Tracking: a code placed on a "thank you"/confirmation page allowing you to track and monitor the number of leads or sales gained from the number of impressions

Content Advertising: ads on web pages of site owners participating in and signing up for split commission services

CPA: "Cost-Per-Acquisition" is the amount you pay as a percentage of how many leads you get from a pay-per-click ad campaign

CPC: "Cost-Per-Click" is the amount of money you will pay for a single click on a pay-per-click advertising campaign

CPM: "Cost-Per-Thousand" describes ads that are charged a certain amount for every 1,000 impressions the ad receives

CTR: "Click-Through-Rate" is the number of clicks divided by the number of impressions

Embed: to insert media, an image, or a link to another website into your own website, email, or blog post

Download: to receive data from an outside source (online or from a disk or other hard drive) onto your own hard drive

Export: to transmit data from your server or hard drive to another location either online or on another data port/ hard drive

Field: a section of a website, usually where a user types personal information or selects from a range of options

Google Slap: Google's penalty for advertisers who have landing pages and sites with insufficient content

Homepage: the base of your website, a landing page from which a user can find any other page on your site

HTML: a commonly used website programming/ coding language

Import: to receive data from an outside source onto your own hard drive or computer, similar to downloading

Impressions: an advertisement's appearance on an accessed Web page, used to measure the number of views an ad receives

Keywords: search terms your customers would use to find your business or service, can be exact and/ or broad

Leads: potential customers

Link: a way for browsers to connect directly from your website to another website, a part of HTML code

Micro-blogging: another term for Twitter, posting short blog messages

Opt-in: a process that allows consumers to decide how much contact they want from your company in the form of emails

Optimization: designing your website so that search engines and web browsers can find it quickly, putting your company high on their lists

Page Rank: also "rank", the order in which your site appears on a search result list

Parent Site: a website that hosts a page for you, generally with specific media, but that is linked to your own website (e. g. Vimeo.com, Blogspot.com)

Post: to self-publish a message, either on a blog or on a discussion board

Profile: a personalized page on a social media site, like a personal website, but part of a larger network, with a pre-designed, limited format

Quality Score: a search engine's score for your landing page and your advertising copy used in your pay-per-click campaign

Query: when a user enters words into a search engine's search field to find information

ROI: Return on Investment

Search Engine: a program on the Internet that allows users to search for information

Search Partners: a search engine related to a larger search engine but with a more specific function (searching for video, images, etc.)

Searchability: how easy it is for people to find your site in a search engine, related to your page rank on any search engine

SMS: "Short Message Service", another term for a text message

Streaming: playing audio or video immediately as it is downloaded from the Internet, rather than storing it in a file on the receiving computer first.

Subdomain: a form of your website URL that allows users to access your site either on a mobile device or from another method

Traffic/Trafficked: the amount of people searching any website, including how many different users and how many repeat viewers.

Twitter: to post mico-blogs to the Twitter website, usually done from a mobile device

Tweets: individual Twitter messages

Upload: similar to exporting, uploading is putting content or data from your computer or hard drive online, usually a large document or some form of multi-media

URL: "Uniform Resource Locator" (formerly Universal Resource Locator) is an Internet address that tells a browser where to find an Internet resource

Web Analytics: the study of how people navigate the internet, which can measure how effective your advertising campaign is

Webseries: video content produced and broadcast online

Widget: a button or small icon that links to another site or opens a pop-up window to take you to another application

Vlog: a video blog, usually filmed with a webcam, a very simple online video

REFERENCES

Section 1

1. Neilson Reports figures, WebVisible.com, March 2009
2. SM+B survey, www.yourseoplan.com, May 2009
3. ibid.
4. S. G. Cowen & Co. figures, April 2009
5. ibid.
6. ibid.
7. www.AOL.com, May 2009

Section 2

1. Direct Marketing Association figures
2. Ogilvy Ad Research figures

Section 3

1. Vocus Whitepaper
2. www.paidcontent.org, March 2009
3. Businessweek.com, "The Myspace Generation." March 2009
4. ADAGE.com, March 9. 2009

Section 4

1. http://adage.com/mobilemarketingguide.08/ April 2009

SPECIAL BONUS!!!!

As part of your purchase, you are given access to our exclusive members area. Each week a new article will be published on a specific topic to help your business grow.

LEARN MORE

Secrets to Free Advertising on the Internet

Your online advertising campaign doesn't just end with this book. We'll give you continued guidance, extensive resources, and a MEMBERS ONLY website where you can find top secret tips that every business owner should know.

www.RobertNoll.com

BUY A SHARE OF THE FUTURE IN YOUR COMMUNITY

These certificates make great holiday, graduation and birthday gifts that can be personalized with the recipient's name. The cost of one S.H.A.R.E. or one square foot is $54.17. The personalized certificate is suitable for framing and will state the number of shares purchased and the amount of each share, as well as the recipient's name. The home that you participate in "building" will last for many years and will continue to grow in value.

Here is a sample SHARE certificate:

Sample certificate reads:
HABITAT FOR HUMANITY
THIS CERTIFIES THAT
__YOUR NAME HERE__
HAS INVESTED IN A HOME FOR A DESERVING FAMILY
1985-2005
TWENTY YEARS OF BUILDING FUTURES IN OUR COMMUNITY ONE HOME AT A TIME
1200 SQUARE FOOT HOUSE @ $65,000 = $54.17 PER SQUARE FOOT
This certificate represents a tax deductible donation. It has no cash value.

YES, I WOULD LIKE TO HELP!

I support the work that Habitat for Humanity does and I want to be part of the excitement! As a donor, I will receive periodic updates on your construction activities but, more importantly, I know my gift will help a family in our community realize the dream of homeownership. **I would like to SHARE in your efforts against substandard housing in my community!** *(Please print below)*

PLEASE SEND ME _____ SHARES at $54.17 EACH = $ $_____

In Honor Of: _____

Occasion: (Circle One)   HOLIDAY   BIRTHDAY   ANNIVERSARY

      OTHER: _____

Address of Recipient: _____

Gift From: _____   *Donor Address:* _____

Donor Email: _____

I AM ENCLOSING A CHECK FOR $ $_____ PAYABLE TO HABITAT FOR HUMANITY OR PLEASE CHARGE MY VISA OR MASTERCARD *(CIRCLE ONE)*

Card Number _____   Expiration Date: _____

Name as it appears on Credit Card _____   Charge Amount $ _____

Signature _____

Billing Address _____

Telephone # Day _____   Eve _____

PLEASE NOTE: Your contribution is tax-deductible to the fullest extent allowed by law.
Habitat for Humanity • P.O. Box 1443 • Newport News, VA 23601 • 757-596-5553
www.HelpHabitatforHumanity.org

Printed in the USA
CPSIA information can be obtained
at www.ICGtesting.com
JSHW052018140824
68134JS00027B/2529